SHOWCASES

By Dorothea Straus

Thresholds
Showcases

Dorothea Straus

SHOWCASES

Boston

HOUGHTON MIFFLIN COMPANY

1974

Library of Congress Cataloging in Publication Data
Straus, Dorothea.   Showcases.
A novel.   I. Title.
PZ4.S9133Sh   [PS3569.T6918]   813'.5'4   74–8577
ISBN 0–395–19423–7

Printed in the United States of America

*To all my showcases—past, present,
and, perhaps, future.*

"It is the tragedy of other people that they
are merely the showcases for the very perish-
able collections of our own mind."

Marcel Proust
Remembrance of Things Past
The Sweet Cheat Gone

Preface

The museum is located at one of those intersections of New York City where two distinct neighborhoods, foreign to each other, adjoin. Out of the north, Harlem presses the staid apartment houses of upper Fifth Avenue. These face Central Park, stretching in a dimming vista as far as the eye can see. Here, at the museum, they end. The building is dedicated to the preservation of the history of the city.

I am startled on entering to be greeted by three coffins: three fallen columns — white, gray, and one made of un-painted boards. Along with a bold poster proclaiming: FIGHT DRUGS, *they form the introduction to a current exhi-bition. A blown-up photograph of a giant syringe points at the door like a cannon, a reminder that the leisurely pursuit of the past is likely to be interrupted by the explosive, oblivi-ous present.*

Yet on the second floor the historical displays are serene. Behind glass, the life-size model rooms (eighteenth, nine-teenth, and early twentieth century) are perfect in every detail: colonial furniture evolving into the intricacies of imported Renaissance decor — austerity giving way to new riches. All of it is familiar but ghostly, like the remnant of a dream losing reality at the arrival of a new day. (Downstairs, at the drug exhibition, the loudspeaker can be heard denouncing the evils of heroin and morphine.) In their period settings, the wax dummies are expressionless: a Puritan family, some Civil War belles, a railroad heiress. Their authentic costumes are contrasting, but their bland pink faces are identical. No item is overlooked. In the early settler's home, a stuffed squirrel is forever nibbling from a dish of nuts beneath a pine-board table and, in the turn-of-the-century parlor, the ceiling crowded with cherubs has been lifted from an Italian palazzo, while the spangled gown encasing the vast sloping bosom of the dummy was donated from the wardrobe of a New York City dowager.

In the adjoining hall the models are smaller but no less detailed. Early shipping is represented by colorful scenes in glass boxes. The first shows the discovery of New York City harbor. The Indians are welcoming the arrival with benign dignity, calmly unaware of their ultimate fate — which is not depicted in the exhibition. The history of Wall Street is also reproduced with doll-house accuracy: the simple beginning looks like a village outing. The display moves through several stages toward an early twentieth-century scene of the stock exchange, in which frock-coated gentlemen with high stiff collars are clustered around a ticker-tape machine which drops its paper messages around the room in fluttering confusion, like a swarm of white pigeons. The second floor is silent and vacant, while downstairs an awed crowd shuffles through the gallery of drugs. Dark faces are rapt as church-goers, while the loudspeaker, with the voice of an old-time preacher, continues to boom out warnings concerned with the punishment and perils of this newest version of hell.

Museum showcases preserve the past in endurable matter, but they cannot catch the essences of other days — only memory can do this. Memory is capricious and evanescent, subject to alteration by circumstances and surroundings and linked to the body's mortality. It is inaccurate and disproportionate, enlarging a small incident or minor character, while important events may be obliterated. Yet I place my faith in it and follow where it leads into the maze of the imagination. Museum showcases merely honor history in funereal displays of dead wax behind glass, but the collections of my mind can be quickened to sudden life. They are the gifts from another, magical world not yet destroyed by time.

SHOWCASES

Early Gods

SOMETIMES FROM MY BED in the early morning, half awake, I hear the evocative cry of sea gulls above the drone of New York City traffic. "Cree, cree, cree-ee," the gulls are calling, unabashed by the whirring, masticating noise made by the maw of a garbage truck and the competitive shriek of a siren. Among the skyscrapers I can picture the white swooping wings. Are they lost? Did they fly too far inland? Or are my ears leading me across Manhattan Island to the docks where the gulls are ushering in an ocean liner — a rare occurrence these days? In my mind's eye I can see the giant gleaming smokestacks banded with stripes of red, blue, or yellow, like summer play clothes. I can smell the familiar odors of linoleum and polished brass that accompanied the crossings of my childhood. A chant of old ships' names passes through my head: *Bremen, Europa, Normandie, Ile de France, Mauretania, Berengaria* — a list of dinosaurs. Then Lynn Fontanne and Alfred Lunt make their reappearance, emerging from clouds of forgetfulness.

I had been sitting with my family in the Palm Lounge of the *Berengaria*, which had not yet steamed out of Southampton. The summer's journey had been accomplished once again. Our traveling company — my parents, my brother and I, Tini the French maid, Mademoiselle the governess, and my brother's tutor — had trailed through Paris, Munich, Vienna, Milan, London. We had halted by the side of a lake, beneath the Alps, at the seashore. Had we, perhaps, impressed some trace of ourselves on a narrow street or a flower-strewn meadow? Would our footprints, washed away by the waves, become part of the composition of some pebbly beach? I liked to think that our strenuous travel had left some mark in its wake. But when I climbed the gangplank and was re-engulfed in the colossal ship's interior, our journeys fell away and my thoughts bounded across the Atlantic toward home, school, the beginning of a fresh year. Summer holidays were interruptions in the business of living, and the ship was a hyphen between the unreality of travel and the reality of home.

On these travels, staring at fellow tourists, making stories from their appearance constituted my chief pastime. I was especially susceptible to royalty. I recall a lunch at a seaside hotel in France where my family was summering. I see a big glass room like a conservatory. The wine steward, resembling a medieval guild master with his long gold chain, had just received my father's order when, reverently closing the menu and bending low conspiratorially, he whispered, "Monsieur, the Prince of Wales is seated at your left." The name had a magical connotation and in no time I located my object: an old-young man with fair hair and perky Peter Pan features in a prematurely wizened face, withered, perhaps, by the sun or the harsh light of too much fame. What I could see of him above the table was slim to the point of frailness. He was wearing tweeds and I guessed that beneath the table his royal legs were encased in knickers like those my father wore for golfing. His attire was a disappointment, for I had expected a crown perhaps a size smaller than the King's, an ermine cape, and purple velvet. But as I stared, his silver gilt hair became a royal headgear, and the ordinary hotel dining room chair, a duplicate of the one I was sitting on myself, was transformed into a mighty throne.

Not long ago I read the Duke of Windsor's obituary. The newspaper portrait showed the same face, young-old now, naturally more wizened, but with the same Peter Pan features. But the image no longer conjured up crown or throne; instead, a forlorn member of café society appeared to have been lodging these many years inside the person of the former Prince of Wales and King.

Another summer my father took the cure in Karlsbad, a place I particularly loathed, for the Cure House had a stupefying hospital atmosphere. Attached to it was an enclosed promenade where the patients who had eaten and drunk too much during the rest of the year strolled up and down sipping tepid sulphurous cure water from etched Bohemian glasses while they concentrated on the vagaries of their intestinal tracts. The hotel was even worse. There the orchestra was perpetually playing popular tunes, and I felt melancholy because I was without a partner. I even envied the very old, the bedizened widows and rouged divorcées I observed on the dance floor. At least they were being led into the intricate steps of the tango, waltz, or fox trot by the three hotel gigolos: one dark, one blond, one with a shiny bald pate, like the three wicked princes in a fairy tale.

There was nothing for me to do to while away the dull hours. One day our French maid, Tini, reported that ex-King Alphonso of Spain was taking the cure, living nearby in a rented villa. She related, furthermore, that the natives believed he was unlucky, the possessor of the evil eye. Like a black cat he must never be allowed to cross one's path. For me his image was heightened by superstition. His royal blood tainted by hemophilic genes, his exile and his loneliness touched me. When he was pointed out, his stooped height, swarthy complexion, aristocratically hooked nose, and pendulous lower lip showed him to be a proper Bourbon. One afternoon Tini, my brother, and I were strolling along Karlsbad's main shopping street — a costly bazaar — when the sidewalk was suddenly emptied, people scuttling inside the stores like ants under rocks. King Alphonso was advancing toward us dressed like any tourist with a camera slung from his shoulder. He seemed impervious to the effect he was producing; proud and unflinching, he bore his stigma royally. When our paths crossed I thought his eyes met mine. For me his glance carried no ill luck; rather, dispelling my boredom, it elevated me like the ritual tap of a royal scepter.

Now, in the lounge of the *Berengaria* on this particular home voyage, I eyed the passengers trapped in this transitional world with me. I knew that before we docked many of their faces would have become familiar, but when we dispersed along the New York City docks I would not meet them again. The ship was a nation in microcosm, with its own population, customs, and climate. My father was reading the passenger list aloud to the rest of us and I was hoping it would include some families with children with whom I could share this seven-day life span — when suddenly he stopped and, looking up from his reading, said, "There go the Lunts." The name meant nothing to me, but following my father's glance, I saw a couple moving arm in arm across the lounge. They were of indeterminate age. Her step was sinuous, flowing — his, purposeful. Her houri's black eyes in a lily-white face were expressionless, almost unseeing, yet replete with some sensuous secret of their own. His eyes took in the surroundings mockingly, with arrogance. I took note of all this, but I would have been incapable of describing the Lunts at that moment, though my observation of them was as intense as a Peeping Tom's. This initial sight of the famous actor-couple, Lynn Fontanne and Alfred Lunt, gave me a sensation of *déjà vu*. Romantic love, even so early a species as mine, is a preform embedded in the imagination. And the object that sparks it is the form it has been waiting for. So perfectly do the two fit that the instant of recognition is like something we have lived through before. What caused me, a ten-year-old girl, to fasten on this middle-aged theatrical pair? This attraction, androgynous and un-requited, was to remain as much a mystery as later more realized ones — creatures of the imagination, all — rooted in obscurity and branching into multifaceted brilliance, yet destined for transformation and eventual extinction, like the fugitive moment itself.

Shipboard existence was divided into territories in strict accordance with the clock that crept back a bit each day, so that upon arrival the European hours were dropped, dis-solved in the foaming wake of sea water. And when we docked on the other side we would assume the new time like a mantle of protective coloring. In the morning I awoke in my cabin to the flat light of the porthole, through whose round eye I could see a blank view of alternating sea and sky. I listened to the washing swish of waves, the protesting groan of hinges, the creaking of steamer trunks fastened to the floor and felt the mild caressing puffs of salt air. Later, the hours spent on the promenade deck were reminiscent of the life at European spas that I had left without regret. Gentlemen in tweed knickers and peaked caps and ladies in white flannel with floppy felt hats or close-fitting cloches marched around and around, the same ones appearing and disappearing like horses in a carousel. Or they lay stretched out on their deck chairs, tucked into plaid blankets like patients at a sanitorium. At noon, promptly, announced by a blast from the foghorn, consommé and crackers appeared, passed around by stewards like hospital attendants and consumed by their charges in self-absorbed obedience. At five in the afternoon, the same ritual was repeated, but tea and ginger snaps were substituted. And the light on the white-capped waves had altered from blatant midday to the mobile, subtle shadings that were prelude to another night. Meals in the vast gilded dining room were also punctuating marks, as were the movies in the lounge and ring tennis and shuffleboard on the upper deck, the only place directly exposed to fresh air. The rest of the ship was as enclosed as any *hôtel splendide,* and the sight of the ocean outside panes of thick glass was no more real than the landscapes hanging on the walls of our rooms at the Ritz, Palace, Continental, or Bristol — through which we had passed on our travels. Ship routine was immensely boring and the blended smells of linoleum, brass polish, and salt air made me queasy. The slow, pitching motion that weighted one's feet at one step and lifted the next to giddy weightlessness added to the malaise.

In our group, only my father was well at all times. Even during a storm, when the waves swelled in leaden anger and the rest of us were laid low in our cabins or pretending to be well on deck while we made nervous calculations about the behavior of our stomachs and the heaving sea outside, my father's small, compact person seemed to defy the elements. His step over a raised iron threshold was as sprightly as ever, his swarthy, smooth-shaven face never lost its glow, and his bow tie remained at just the correct angle. On bad days he would even eat a many-course meal in the deserted dining room, heartlessly reciting the menu to us afterwards, enjoy a strong cigar in the smoking lounge or attend a tipsy showing of a movie in the Palm Court. Though uncomfortable, these storms were not exciting and boredom held us fast. We seemed to be obeying, in sedated submission, the ship's routine that kept us all so busy doing nothing.

Before my father's innocent remark, "There go the Lunts," I had no inkling that this return voyage on the *Berengaria* would be any different from its predecessors. But from that moment to the moment of my reluctant disembarkation, my life was to have purpose. The *art nouveau* lounges were transformed into stage sets for the glamorous presences of Lynn Fontanne and Alfred Lunt. The potted palms, brass railings, grand staircase, and folding deck chairs were magical properties — and the curtain had just gone up. I was in love.

I estimated that the Lunts would be late risers, so starting about noon on our first day out, skillfully evading Mademoiselle and the company of my brother, I began my search. I was rewarded because I soon came upon Lynn Fontanne and Alfred Lunt rounding a corner of the promenade deck. She was wearing a turban that hid her black hair and accentuated her eyes and scarlet lips. The beautiful effect of her face appeared to be an achievement of art more than nature. Under her chin, a flowing bow was tied like a ribbon to a hothouse plant. They were again arm in arm and he was still looking about him with that gaze, both ironic and conquering. He was a tall man with an imposing silhouette, but he could not have been called handsome. His dark hair, sleek as patent leather, was parted in the center, his nose was large and slightly hooked, his lips, thick. At that second encounter I was forced to revise the memory of my first glimpse of them which I had been hoarding overnight. The new view, though different, was no less fascinating and the lightning alteration was delightful work. I reversed my direction on the deck to follow them as closely as I dared, and, for the first time, I heard their voices — the famous voices of the Lunts, familiar to their audiences but new to me, became my miraculous finding.

By this time I had gathered some information about them. She was English, he from Wisconsin, of Scandinavian extraction. She spoke with a British accent and a melodic teasing lilt. His speech was fluent, guttural, with a faintly foreign intonation. I was close enough to benefit from this duet, as moving to my ears as a dialogue between violin and piano. I do not know how many times I circled the deck, at a safe distance, like a sleuth. At length they turned inside and, never losing them from sight, I followed as they descended into the maze of corridors. I spied them as they entered their cabin, and with the door closed between us I made an important discovery: their cabin number was forty-seven, B Deck; Valhalla had been located.

When we gathered for our first lunch, I was abstracted, ignoring Mademoiselle's constant low-toned instructions in French, my father's familiar jokes, my brother's noisy monologues, and the perpetually anxious expression on my mother's lovely transparent face. Even my habitual curiosity about my fellow passengers had been neutralized. And though Mademoiselle was obliged to utter her usual remonstrances — *"Assieds-toi droite — ne mets pas tes coudes sur la table — tiens tes yeux sur ton assiette"* — I was not looking for possible playfellows, nor staring at the ladies' costumes, but continuing my search for the Lunts. I could no longer remember a time when this had not been my preoccupation. They did not appear and the meal was wasted. But I felt cheerful and optimistic. They could not escape the ship and the morning had added to their image many fascinating details that I would sort out later at my leisure.

I collected glimpses of Alfred Lunt and Lynn Fontanne from various parts of the ship. And those places where they had been became special, worthy of my notice even after they were no longer there. In my intensity I never stopped to wonder whether the Lunts noticed me — their shadow — skinny-legged, in golf socks, with scabby knees and round eyes, memorizing their renewed but shifting charms. My secret pleasure was a talisman against melancholy. Once I had envied the couples gyrating at the tea-dance hour when everyone seemed to have found someone else. Now I no longer wished that my chronic state of childhood would end so that I too might be whirled about by my partner — my face bored and sophisticated, my limbs rhythmic and nimble

— to the strains of "The Beautiful Blue Danube" or "Who." Music made me dream, but until now it had only produced longings for some vague future. Sometimes on our travels, the hypnotic clatter of the train running across some foreign countryside at night evolved into a remembered snatch of song. And I would feel that I was being hurtled toward a featureless stranger waiting for me with his arms wide open. But when I looked out of the window, I was met merely by my own reflection against a chain of jiggling railroad lights.

Before long I learned that the Lunts did not eat in the main dining room, but in the small Veranda Café on the top deck. This had been a disappointment, although it seemed fitting that they should not be exposed to the commotion and ostentation of shipboard meals. They belonged in their intimate, glass-enclosed showcase with what I supposed to be a chosen élite. They dined late and my evenings were spent haunting the top deck, circling the Veranda Café like a night moth. On one occasion, I did not find them at their table and I climbed a ladder, higher, to where the smokestacks rose like Roman pillars, at once ghostly and solid, their white paint washed by shadows and moonlight. Along the deck, the lifeboats reminded me of mummies, swathed in canvas and bound by ropes. Only the sound of gently breaking waves, far below, broke the silence. Suddenly I saw two shapes cut out against a smokestack. Had my thoughts, like a magic lantern, conjured them up? He was impeccable in his tuxedo, she was wearing a long, gauzy white dress with wings sprouting from her shoulders. Diamond pendants swung from her ears like constellations. Slowly, as though directed from outside, the figures came together. Two sleek, dark heads merged and the double shadow was magnified hugely against the smokestack. When they separated, I did not follow but sat down weakly at the vacated spot. Had the scene been real or imagined? To this day I cannot be sure. But the moonlit vision was mine, along with the instinctive desire for its preservation. Yet it was to be obliterated in time, until the coarse cry of sea gulls returned it to me intact across the intervening city and the unrolling of the years.

It was the sea gull's cry also that announced our arrival as the *Berengaria* moved slowly into harbor, nudged into its berth by the tugboats that worried its leviathan sides like swarming gnats. I had watched, with apathy, the unusually heady appearance of the Statue of Liberty and the rise of the New York skyline, proclaiming both hope and menace, like a cluster of gigantic Druid stones.

Now our group was gathered in the Palm Lounge once more, ready for disembarkation. My father was dressed again in a business suit; my mother was nervously burrowing in the depths of her bulky bag, as though searching for the last time for passport, smelling salts, and the playing cards she used for solitaire on our train trips — those traveling staples no longer necessary until summer came again. Tini was sitting with her plump, work-callused hands folded on her lap, uncharacteristically idle, Mademoiselle was still issuing orders and her neck had turned a coxcomb red, due to the excitement of landing. My brother's tutor seemed to be already severed from our circle, as he would be returning to his college — his role with us was only summer stock. My brother, having collected all the literature on the Cunard Line for his pamphlet collection, was on deck, watching us nose into port. And I, usually impatient to get off, to find again the lost treasures of the winter season — books, toys left behind, friends, and school — was clinging to the ship during those last minutes and experiencing the jagged pangs of parting. I longed for one more glimpse of the Lunts. I was nostalgic for that moment, a lifetime ago, when I had first seen them in the Palm Lounge.

"Since we are all ready, we might as well go up on deck," my father ordered, taking charge of his troop for the last time. We followed his lead, I scanning the crowd in vain. We inched our way to the gangplank. Ordinarily, I felt important, exultant, as I marched down its steep incline toward the upturned faces on the dock. I was an awaited emissary returning from a foreign mission. But today, my heart was leaden and my step reluctant. I alone knew the secret of what I was leaving behind on the abandoned ship. My disembarking was an act of double disloyalty.

On the wharf the air was stale and sooty and it was difficult to breathe after the clean salt breezes of the crossing. We moved with the crowd toward the custom inspection shed, finding our place beneath the letter L. I was sitting on the edge of a steamer trunk, dangling my legs, when I spotted the Lunts. How could I have overlooked the startling fact that their name, also, began with L? They too were dressed in city clothes. She was again adorned with a floppy bow under her chin — blue and white polka dots — and a turban to match. She was following his stride with that sinuous motion that was her trademark. Their progress through the groups of weary travelers waiting for inspection should have been heralded by an operatic overture. I prayed that we would not be obliged to leave before they did. Thank heavens, we were many and our luggage numerous. My father was still busy collecting all the pieces when the Lunts moved up to an inspector. I savored the moment. A look inside their bags would be an act of intimacy and, also, an archeological discovery. An open suitcase was overflowing with a pile of crumpled shirts, no different from my father's used linen, but for this very reason significant. Under the shirts, I detected some shoes and a dark glass bottle. Lynn Fontanne was unfastening her vanity case, revealing rows of jars and flacons with pink enamel tops — liquids, unguents, paints, the raw materials for the composing of her face.

I was so lost in my investigations that I failed to notice that Alfred Lunt was approaching me until he was standing beside the steamer trunk on which I was sitting. In a flash, I took in his face, closer than it had ever been before. The heavy, quizzically raised eyebrow, the yellow eyes like a fox, the hooked nose, the full lips. I seemed to see every pore in his skin with unnatural clarity. For the first time, his eyes met mine, took note of my presence, as in slow motion his lips parted to speak to me. Was this to be the reward for my adoration? Had my cloud of invisibility failed me? Perhaps the Lunts had been aware of me all along, only pretending not to see me. And now that we were about to disperse, he thought it safe to talk to me — a famous actor condescending to a fan, a middle-aged man addressing a little girl. No, this was not to be the meager climax to my love. I would keep it unspoiled, as perfect as I had made it. I would not permit reality to damage it. Jumping down from my perch, I ran off, leaving Alfred Lunt standing there, his banal, rejected words unuttered.

My one-sided love affair with the Lunts did not end here.

It was a triangle, with only one line — myself — drawn; the other sides formed a lofty pinnacle, but they were traced in invisible ink. Upon my return to New York, my way of life on board the *Berengaria* was left behind and I moved into a new phase. In reversal of a real love relationship, proximity was the first stage, to be followed by admiration at a distance. I was introduced to the theater world of the Lunts.

For several seasons I fervently followed their appearances on stage, often part of a row of schoolgirls celebrating a birthday at a matinée. No one divined the state of my heart. I would watch the Lunts disporting themselves behind the footlights — early gods at play. How sophisticated and artful they were, yet how fleshy, with a sly sexuality that was all the more inflammatory because of its deviousness. Today I sometimes think of them as I sit unmoved before a stage or screen writhing with nudity — grubby, blatant, yet clinical and sexless. The Lunts, deities themselves, had the gift for evoking the mischievous god.

I attended all their plays as many times as I could manage it. I learned the history of their career — its beginning (before my birth) in widely separated Wisconsin and London, their coming together in New York, their marriage and their joint successes. It was mythology, and then the gods materialized in human form, graciously allowing me to be witness to their sport on earth. Even the titles of their plays had magic, and in a shoe box I saved all the programs. On the covers were photographs of the Lunts in costumes and in modern clothes, full length, facing front or in profile, but always together, like a Janus-headed coin. I would study them in the privacy of my room, but when I saw them on stage I was always obliged to reconstruct them. The mobile image gained intensity behind the footlights, under layers of grease paint. How I drank in the suggestiveness of his prowl, his well-known voice, guttural, wide in range, rich in implication, with its trace of Scandinavian accent — and her body, fluid, seemingly boneless, and her long white throat that swiveled like a swan's. At the end of the play they would step forward to take their bows, hand in hand. They faced the audience as they had me, on the *Berengaria,* looking at us without seeing us. In the dark of the theater, I would experience the returning thrill. I was again the Peeping Tom absorbing each alluring detail, without fear of detection. One season, as Prince Rudolf of Hapsburg, Alfred Lunt played a seduction scene with Lynn Fontanne. The fact that they were actually husband and wife added to my titillation. He would bend amorously over the back of a sofa where she lay extended in clinging white satin, raising her glass of champagne to his. Piecing together my memories with what I could discern on the stage, I saw his raised eyebrow, his sentient glance, her dark eyes with their depth of secrets, guarded by sweeping artificial lashes. Their voices blended, teasing and erotic, with a questioning inflection that required no answer but the meeting of two bodies. No matter that the curtain always came down to intercept them — their unconcluded games satisfied me.

In time I lost my early wisdom; I longed to meet Alfred Lunt and Lynn Fontanne. My mother and father had a friend, "Uncle Victor," a failed concert pianist and music teacher, a mild, blue-eyed, balding, middle-aged homosexual. But he had glamour for me. He knew the Lunts. At my parents' dinner parties he was frequently an "extra man," and I begged to attend and to be allowed to sit next to him. Using every blandishment I could muster, I wheedled him into promises of an introduction. But several years passed, the programs in the shoe box multiplied, and the meeting never took place. Slowly, imperceptibly, I stopped caring. I still went to see them act, but the excitement had dwindled. I was preoccupied, hunting for my former self and the emotions that had relinquished me before I was ready to relinquish them. I had been expelled from that world, born, in an instant, in the Palm Court of the *Berengaria*. Now, in a different incarnation, I was on the verge of new creations.

Not long ago, in the crowded elevator of a store, I saw the Lunts again. By this time their age was legendary and they had retired to their farm in Wisconsin. How often in my childhood I had attempted to picture this domesticated Valhalla. It appeared to me both rural and theatrical, with a well-appointed kitchen, where he played master chef, and, in a garden, a wisteria-draped gazebo with a *chaise longue*. The figure of Rudolf of Hapsburg, in full dress military regalia, was perpetually bending toward Lynn Fontanne, who lay stretched out in an unsuitable white satin evening gown, while a string orchestra played Viennese waltzes and champagne glittered in the moonlight — the same moonlight that also bathed the wide fields and silos of the Wisconsin farmlands . . . In the elevator I could only catch sight of their backs, still side by side. He was white-haired, she, henna-dyed, in a scarlet raincoat. They were stooped, sadly diminished. But, loyal to that other self, I pushed my way with the old expertise toward a better view of them. Four eyes met mine, unchanged — his interrogating, arrogant ones, her houri black ones, still fringed with long artificial lashes. It was I who looked away first, as though I were apologizing — to whom and for what, I did not know.

CHAPTER II

Harlequinade

A FIRST LOVE AFFAIR is sudden shock. I examine with awe the zaniness of mine, now so long over, and view its irrational particulars like points of light salvaged from the black backdrop of forgetfulness. And I see that it had forerunners in the more distant past like a dress rehearsal before the curtain's rising.

It began with Albert, the herald, later servitor to the leading player. In my senior year in high school Albert had been passed around from girl to girl, always the victim of unrequited love. We all gained power from his abject protestations and he too seemed to profit from his invariably hopeless suit. Now I realize that Albert's humble passage among us was meant to deceive us and possibly himself, too. It was like a disguise to mask his oddly soft, seemingly boneless person. He had a round head topped by a fuzz of brown hair, a round face with round features. He resembled a bumblebee and like one he hovered around us, magnetized but volatile, skimming from flower to flower with the lightest contact possible.

My turn came in the spring. Now friends listened to my tales of Albert. To us he was an "older man," already at law school, which compensated for his bizarre appearance. Graduation was a flurry of white dresses down the aisle of the auditorium. My self-importance was increased because I was aware that somewhere in the audience Albert was seeking me out exclusively. After the ceremony I remember the poison green of the lawn around the Westchester house my parents had rented for the summer. I took voluptuous pleasure in the smell of the new grass, the prospect of the long idle hours of vacation, and the recently acquired consciousness of my own charms, as Albert followed in the wake of my swaying white skirt. That evening I recall that I lay stretched out on the cool grass beside a picket fence while Albert stood on the opposite side gazing at me with exaggerated rapture. I closed my eyes, testing my power to attract, and swiftly, obediently, in silence, Albert jumped the fence and landed on top of me with surprising weightlessness. I brushed him off and moved away confident that he would be following close behind.

I no longer remember how that particular summer fled, but back in the city in the fall I found myself with Albert at a nightclub. His homage had grown perfunctory and I was frankly bored. I was waiting for something I did not know.

"I hope you won't object," Albert was saying. "I asked a friend from Yale to join us here." His words had no warning in them. In the claustrophobic dimness I watched the nightclub act. Near the ceiling someone was swinging on a trapeze crisscrossed by floodlights. It was 1934 and the nightclubs in New York were making up in lavishness for the greater popularity and lawlessness of the vanished speak-easies. I was wearing a deep blue evening dress shot with silver thread and its faintly metallic odor would return to me later when I thought of the Flying Trapeze and Skinny's dazzling entrance there.

That night I would not have been capable of describing him. Like all bright objects he was revealed bit by bit. At the time of our meeting he consisted mainly of the pounding of my own heart and the oblique dramatic lighting of the Flying Trapeze. Now I am able to reconstruct his appearance: unnaturally tall and slender, with long legs like the blades of shearing scissors; his hair, prematurely gray, in a deep Mephistophelean point on his forehead, as sleek and shining as a silver helmet. He had a long face with regular features and full shapely lips over very white teeth, and the brilliance of his blue, black-fringed eyes was doubled by his steel-rimmed glasses. His voice was electric, slightly high-pitched. When we danced that first night, his body felt brittle but his feet were so nimble that we seemed to be flying higher than the trapeze. We whirled away, and from a great distance I glimpsed Albert's familiar form sitting at the vacated table — a tiny landmark, unregretted, growing unrecognizable as though seen from the dizzy altitude of an airplane.

Afterward, Skinny, Albert, and I were sometimes a threesome. Albert had dropped his disguise and instead of addressing himself to me with overt worship, his small green eyes followed Skinny with surreptitious but unmistakable love. He took vicarious pleasure in the progress of our relationship and, if we happened to be alone, Skinny's name was always on our lips. I asked for nothing better. As for

Skinny, he appeared to ignore Albert's adoration. The humbled bumblebee was part of our natural habitat, living in the climate of our infatuation. Although I was oblivious to it at the time, these two were in direct line from an earlier pair at a school I had attended. The double portrait of Skinny and Albert had fitted inside it — like Chinese boxes — a distant, therefore smaller, version of itself.

The school building consisted of two ramshackle brownstones on the West Side. It was "progressive," so many of the students were odd and considered to be gifted. The faculty observed these incubating talents like diagnosticians following the development of a suspected disease. The Porter twins, Norton and Grover, were exceptions. Blond, blue-eyed, and uncomplicated, they stood out at the Dalton School. Norton, tall and regularly handsome, accepted his brother's homage as a matter of course. Grover was undersized and, although he shared his twin's Nordic coloring, the slight slant of his eyes gave his face an Oriental cast. Norton was a leader — in my memory, perpetually president of the school or athletics captain. Grover, always close by, played a supporting role. He was an after-image, the dancing mote in the eye conceived by looking directly into the sun. From a distance I contemplated Norton's radiance. In assembly I watched him standing in the back row of the chorus (because of his height), singing "All God's Chillun Got Wings," and I tried to single out his voice from the rest. I worked hard to be elected to the student government so that I might serve under his presidency. When I trooped across the covered wooden bridge in the back yard connecting the two houses on my way to a student council meeting, my imagination would leap before me in anticipation of the thud made by the gavel in Norton's hand as he pronounced the magical opening words, "Will the meeting please come to order." He presided at the head of the table and at his right Grover, as secretary, was always to be found bending over the minutes of the day. I was content to worship at a respectful distance and Norton acknowledged my existence by no more than a look or a stray word. Once at the close of a meeting he offered me a piece of chocolate. I accepted it with the solemnity of a marriage vow, treasuring the silver paper wrapper for such a long time that when I finally threw it away I no longer remembered its significance.

Norton Porter, following the Lunts by several years, was their descendant. But I was no longer the sleuth about to flee at the threat of Alfred Lunt's voice addressed to me, dispersing my cloud of invisibility. I had evolved into an ardent serving maid, accepting the offering of milk chocolate with ceremony. Norton Porter, in turn, prefigured Skinny but by then I was ready for the inevitable next step: a first affair.

How can I recapture it? Not long ago on a warm day in May I rested on a bench in Central Park near the Seventy-second Street entrance. I watched the garlanded horses and buggies weighted with their out-of-town tourist fares disappearing at a languid trot around a bend in the road toward the West Side. The brief-blooming dogwood trees were dropping their blossoms across the grass and pavement in a white bridal shower. On the opposite side of the drive, a raised playground swarmed with children climbing over and under a grove of metal devices that looked like instruments of torture. Was it possible that this very spot had been the site of the old Casino-in-the-Park? I tried to conjure up its ghostly presence. Above the children's cries I listened for the sweet low strains of Eddie Duchin's band and the sound of his piano. They evaded me, like Cole Porter's songs recorded by Bobby Short, unrecognizably translated and fragmented into the idiom of today. But sometimes, unexpectedly, unchanged from the past, the lilting moan of "Night and Day" or the sophisticated crowing of "You're the Top" will startle me. Then words and music trap me in their mesh and through it, like the vision of some mythological temple of love, the Casino-in-the-Park arises in my memory.

In my mind's eye the Casino is a circular building with windows all around. The gyrating figures fox-trotting inside must have looked to outsiders like exotic fish in a tank — gaudy and witless — swimming in an atmosphere of artificial warmth. The open noisy playground that has replaced the Casino is, surely, more suited to a public park. But in those days, with Skinny by my side, I was selfishly unaware that tea dancing might be a mockery in the midst of the shuffling, straggling army of the unemployed who used Central Park as headquarters. Saturday afternoons belonged to us. How identical they were, yet how unique each minute. I cannot recall even the smallest scrap of our dialogue, but I can still faintly feel — rather than see — the bright nimbus that surrounded Skinny, causing me at each meeting to struggle to penetrate his face. I saw clearly only outer details: the ruby ring he always wore on the little finger of his left hand, the dapper angle of his stiff-brimmed pearl gray felt hat. In my sight, the ring was as conspicuous as a bull's eye. I pretended to consider it in bad taste while I was, in fact, grateful for it. It reminded me that the gods have their small vanities too. But what I remember best is the dancing. We seemed to have been perpetually whirling and twirling, I held up by Skinny's firm hold and the shared rhythm of our bodies. At night, during the holidays — and from here, the holidays seem to have swallowed up all the other days — there were balls. How extraordinary they look now: the long stag line in swallowtails and white ties considering the girls on the polished floor like purchasers inspecting young heifers on market day. The preparations that took place beforehand might have caused my mirror to crack from boredom as I stood long hours before it, laved, curried, painted — each night a fresh ball gown exhibiting shoulders, bosom, waist just enough to hint at more and better. Every era has its own grotesque customs and rites to celebrate the awakening of sex. But no matter how original the initiates may feel themselves to be, they are united with past generations and those still to come by the sameness of the deity they are celebrating.

Out of the stag line, tall and erect, his silver head topping the rest, Skinny would swoop down on me. Then the familiar vertigo would seize me and the music was for us alone. In a taxi driving home through the Park in the small hours of the morning, I would glimpse the illuminated turrets of the skyscrapers and the less intense light of the stars. Our hands were fiercely intertwined and his ruby ring cut into my flesh, a reminder once again of the mortal conceit of the gods.

Back home, the ritual intensified. The old brocade couch beneath the large somber lithograph of Notre Dame Cathedral was waiting to receive us, inanimate, oblivious, yet by its faithful presence, somehow a collaborator in our lovemaking. In preparation Skinny would remove his steel-rimmed spectacles, slowly, deliberately, extending the longing and anticipation of pleasure. I watched him avidly. With his glasses off, his fair ruddy face looked curiously peeled, revealed in startling nakedness — his eyes diminished and his oval black nostrils and shapely lips magnified. It seemed an act of great intimacy. But soon his face was blotted out in the coming together of our bodies, the preliminary intimacy giving way to a larger, blinder one. After he had gone, I would lie for a long while, unthinking, unfeeling, in my ripped and crumpled ball dress, beneath the lithograph of the dignified enduring façade of Notre Dame.

Our obsession endured for three seasons and, in the way of such attachments, it reduced nature to accessory. The scarlet and golden autumn leaves were his, the enameled snow in Central Park and the pallid green breath of spring. For a while after we had parted, nature's fineries faded into nothingness or, occasionally, a trick of light on leaf or snow would turn into a blade piercing me with longing and regret. But while it lasted, everything was heady, even our brief separations. The sight of his long envelope in my mail box at the college post office was a daily triumph. I would reach for it with the sensuous delight of a fisherman hauling in his catch. The letters were typed and wildly poetic, but the impersonal print was a joy in itself. Meaning, hidden by an impediment of light like Skinny's face, came through to me only after a third or fourth reading. The ringing of the telephone contained his voice and the ticking of the alarm clock next to my bed promised his certain return.

My extravagances were mainly internal. But Skinny's were translated into improvident action. When the gods are at play they assume antic poses. Skinny was both knight and buffoon. I particularly remember an afternoon in New

Haven. Skinny, Albert, and I were wandering about aimlessly. At this period Skinny had begun to broach the topic of marriage and I for some unconscious reason snubbed the idea. Was I unsure of him or not ready yet myself for the next step? Or did I know, instinctively, that such showcases, illumined artificially, must fade in time in the real light of day? At any rate, my "no" sounded like a capricious feint as, rekindled, I watched for his reaction. This day stands out brightly, though inaccurately, in my mind. As we strolled Skinny and I were arguing again about the prospect of marriage. We managed to be unconstrained in the presence of Albert, who remained silent before us. Suddenly Skinny stopped and, flinging up his long arms in a desperate gesture, exclaimed, "If you do not say 'yes' this minute, I'm going to throw myself off that steeple over there!" Albert and I looked in the direction he was indicating at a prim white wooden New England church. Its slanted cottage roof and modest belfry looked innocent enough, unlikely weapons in a suicide for love. But Skinny with pseudo-serious determination was on his way up. Albert and I stood rooted to the spot, imploring him to turn back while we secretly admired the bravura of his performance. When he reached the roof, balancing precariously, Skinny waved a jaunty farewell to us below. Now the church looked miniature while Skinny's silhouette, outsized against the blue sky, resembled one of those fantastic figures floating above a roof-top in a Chagall painting. I called and begged, half-convinced now that he intended to jump. I no longer remember the descent: the film breaks off here and the three of us are arrested in this moment until another scene succeeds it on the screen.

On a night in mid-June, Skinny's twenty-first birthday,

he and I set out to celebrate. We drove into the country to one of those summer theaters that flourished during that time. The top of his convertible was down and our heads were exposed to the cool wind whipped up by our passage along the highway, while our bodies were snugly enclosed, close together, on the warm leather seat. He drove expertly with one hand, and his other arm was draped over my shoulder. My hand rested on the taut slim shaft of his thigh. I always experienced a sense of well-being in Skinny's car; it was a kind of home. The following week I was to go to San Francisco to visit cousins, and Skinny was pressing marriage again — at least an announced engagement before I left. But it was my wish to preserve the present mood — to immobilize the moment. Any change constituted a threat. I remember saying, "Why not use our separation as a trial — both of us free to be with others. After summer, if we still feel the same way — then — maybe . . ." I was confident that separation would only heighten my emotion as it always had and it was unthinkable that anything should be different for Skinny. He argued and I demurred until we reached the theater. I wonder if the breed still exists today — a white silo outlined against the moonlight and the interior still redolent of stable smells. It seemed quite natural to me that the audience in white flannels, blue blazers, and flowered chiffon evening dresses should have evolved from the munching browsing cows in their stalls. As usual, the play was a drawing-room comedy, but I scarcely noticed it, being awake only to the direction of Skinny's hand grazing over me in the dark. At the intermission we moved over the drenched grass to the converted bar that was as rustic and festive as a county fair. On the way back home I was impatient to reach the welcome of the old brocade couch in the library and the overhanging presence of Notre Dame.

For once Skinny did not remove his glasses. I sat on the sofa and he on a chair opposite regarding me in silence. When at last he spoke, his words, though calmly stated, were an explosion: "I don't understand how I could have been taken in by you. We don't speak the same language. You are hard — really unfeeling. Go to California and find someone there of your own kind."

This could not be happening. "But I don't understand. We had such a beautiful evening — and all the while — "

"I thought I might as well go through with it. But now —"

"It can't be true. You must be fooling."

In answer he got up and without another word he was gone. I don't know how long I sat there in the wreckage of the citadel, not knowing if I were alive or dead.

I did not hear from Skinny again but each mail or ring of the telephone was a rising hope brought down. Before my departure for California Albert came to see me. We sat in the library where every inanimate object had come to life in order to torture me. Albert was dressed in a seersucker suit too large for him. It engulfed his small boneless form like a crumpled shopping bag. I noticed that his nose was peeling from sunburn and that he was growing bald. Now he looked more like a malevolent gnome than a humbled bumblebee. He knew our story and we talked of nothing but Skinny. The mention of his name was a pain I eagerly sought. "Skinny has left for the Caribbean on a freighter," Albert told me. "Before he sailed, he bought a gorgeous green parrot to keep him company. I guess it's the only company he wants now."

All the way west I dreamed of Skinny. In spite of the blow, his image was bright — brighter perhaps than ever. I pictured him leaning against a ship's railing, a pipe clamped between his teeth, gazing morosely over a tropical sea — a tall lonely figure with a bright plumed parrot perched on one shoulder. Awareness of the value of the prize gave me strength to bear its loss. But as I sat long hours in the observation car of the *Super Chief,* the wide land fleeing before the train's assault was blurred and the shrill wail of the whistle as we rounded a curve seemed to be issuing from inside me.

In California I worked hard for recovery. But when I allowed myself to be embraced at the close of an evening, it was an unpleasant surprise to discover that the motions were similar to those I had known with Skinny. I had somehow imagined that what we had shared had been our own invention.

The following winter my wounds began to heal. During the Christmas holidays the dances resumed and the penguins in full dress were still appraising from the sidelines. But my actions had become automatic and there was no vertigo. Did I hope to see Skinny? He was there — his silver head topping the rest. When he cut in on my forgotten partner, tapping him lightly on the shoulder with his white-gloved hand, his eyes beamed down into mine from his great height. "Let's get out of here," he said as we danced. "I must talk to you." We fled through the hotel lobby like conspirators. In the taxi he started to explain, "I never meant what I said that night. But you goaded me to it. I was sure you would meet someone in California and I couldn't have stood it." As he went on, I realized my former errors, even my cruelty.

My damaged pride was being restored, but something was wrong, my victory was marred. The gods never explain! They do not suffer from uncertainty and weakness.

When we reached the library, Skinny hurriedly removed his glasses. But his face appeared unchanged without them. He fell on me and I felt his sex rise as though separate from his person. It was as hard as a sword of lath. Even then I knew we were through. Now, looking back from a long distance, our prone sprawling bodies appear like the marionettes in the finale of the puppet shows I used to watch on the Champs-Elysées in my childhood. After rampaging over the miniature stage, Harlequin and Columbine would knock each other down before the curtain was drawn. And I, recovering from my absorption, would follow our French maid back to the hotel where my family was lodged, through the interesting busy streets.

CHAPTER III

Shadow and Substance

THE TREASURES of Paris were spread before me when I was too young. I never possessed even the smallest bit. I was always the tourist looking at the display through a plate glass window.

The Right Bank was our playground bounded by the Seine. Across its bridges, where fishermen seemed to be waiting eternally for their catch, lay the Left Bank, rarely visited by our traveling group. The little I learned about that foreign country came from the reading of French novels. Alexandre Dumas was my favorite. Once in a while I crossed the Pont Neuf to the quays, still known terrain, with their bookstalls and view of the Right Bank. But when I found myself in the bewildering tangle of medieval streets of the Left Bank, the old *hôtels*, tall and grimy with age, like a coterie of haughty aristocrats, seemed to shut out the intruder from the New World. And I would return to the Three Musketeers and their swashbuckling adventures as though to old friends.

It was hard for me to believe — it still is — that once Paris was only this maze of alleys. The vistas formal with statuary, the colonnaded squares, the arcaded streets, the symmetrical parks composed the Paris I had seen first in my infancy. As far back as I can remember, it had been familiar, as though the spokes radiating from the Étoile were part of historical design, the prototype of urban elegance forever. And I had glimpsed it in an earlier incarnation. When my father told me that it was the work of an architect commissioned by Napoleon, I situated the Emperor in a world more antique than the Pharaohs. Even today, it is unthinkable that "my Paris" has not always existed. Yet I have been a stranger there, a sightseer, a voyager without roots. My father delighted in his role, relishing his brief occupancies of expensive hotels, and as he walked briskly along the boulevards he would use his polished cane to point out the sights of interest with enthusiasm undiminished by repetition. His verve could carry me along. But without him Paris produced in me an active melancholy stimulated by its foreign beauty and elusiveness. When I played in the stately Tuileries Gardens or in the elegant intimacy of the Parc Monceau I would pause to marvel at the nimble French chatter of the children rolling hoops or sailing boats near me. How clever they sounded to my ears — how sophisticated! They were at home here, knowing nothing of my vague longing. And I would wish to be accepted by them, to be one of them. But I was separated by the barrier of my nationality as surely as the Seine divided the Right Bank from the Left during those summers long ago.

The only area in which I felt on intimate terms with Paris was inside its railway stations. The names of the terminals were familiar: Gare St. Lazare, Gare Quai d'Orsay, Gare de Lyons, Gare du Nord . . . As I trudged with my family to or from a halted train under a dusty yellowish glass dome of an immense skylight, I was caught up by the excitement of travel. Briefly, I felt that I had conquered Paris. Perhaps this was because in the station there was no pretense of belonging, of being a citizen. Here my tourist status was externalized: the journey and I were one.

After traveling the miles of galleries of the Louvre, I would sometimes buy a reproduction of a painting I had viewed, carrying a Nativity scene or royal portrait back to my hotel room. My parents were gratified, thinking that I had developed a taste for art. But it was only another attempt to capture a portion of the vast grace of Paris, to claim it as my own.

As the visits multiplied and I grew older I lost the small child's gift for observation. The city unrolled itself as a backdrop to my own life. I fell in love in Paris with the man I was to marry. He arrived one day, a friend from the United States, doubly welcome on foreign soil. As we sat together at the Café de la Paix, I listened attentively to the stories of his recent travels through hot Russian cities, companioned by a woman Intourist guide. But by the time he left he was no longer a travel-weary American friend but a shining stranger, who reduced Paris to a nondescript background and the remainder of my summer trip to a series of long days to be lived through somehow until the prize of reunion could be granted. It was in Paris on our honeymoon that news of my mother's sudden death reached us. And the city dwindled into a mere point of departure, a threatening take-off place for my first close encounter with mortality.

After that came World War II, followed by the birth of our son and the establishment of my husband's publishing house. My travels in Europe were discontinued for twenty years. Strangely, during that period Paris was in my thoughts more often than when I had visited it each summer. I would dream of its memorized streets, the expanse of the Place de la Concorde bordered by classical white marble, encircled by rings of fairy light at night — or I would recall a segment of iron filigree, our hotel balcony over which I could see the Eiffel Tower as unreal as a picture postcard of itself across a sea of chestnut trees. Sometimes in New York City when the street cleaners' truck passed by and I saw the asphalt turning dark, I would be back in Paris, newly arrived, at that hour when the streets are still wet from their early morning washing and the metal shutters are lowered like closed eyelids over the fronts of little shops still asleep before the day begins. Paris was in my blood. Still a foreigner to it, I was homesick now for alien places.

I kept in touch with the Paris I remembered by reading Balzac, Maupassant, Proust, and Colette. When my husband became Colette's publisher it was my ambition to meet her, to visit her in her aerie overlooking the gardens of the Palais-Royal. I wanted to see with my own eyes the grand old lady with her kohl-rimmed eyes and hair like a tousled chrysanthemum. I wanted to hear her speech. I felt certain it would carry (as her writing did) the tang of the provinces combined with the language of Parisian music halls, dens, cafés, literary salons, flavored — all of it — by her individual brand of earthy wisdom. I liked to think that all Paris was contained by her. And the wonder was that she was not native. There in her Palais-Royal apartment, though crippled by arthritis, she was a reigning queen, not by birth but by conquest. If we could meet I might at last step across the threshold and lift the barrier that had kept Paris from me for so long. But Colette died before this hope could be realized. On my first visit after twenty years' absence, I could only wander over the silent historical rectangle enclosed by the Palais-Royal, attempting in vain to hear an echo of the Revolutionary mob and, even more, trying to bring back the simple touching speech of the aging shopkeepers waiting out the German occupation during World War II — the obstinate faithful whose dialogue was recorded for all time by Colette, as, always sentient and attentive, she leaned from her window overlooking the courtyard. But nothing remained for me but a brass plaque on the wall, as lifeless and impersonal as a tombstone bearing her name.

My husband and I were asked to dinner by Maurice Goudeket and his new wife, an invitation that once would have caused elation: to be inside a Parisian home, on the other side of the plate glass window! Now I felt disappointment, like a child at Christmas who finds beneath the tree many toys but not the particular one she had wished for. Maurice Goudeket had been Colette's husband, by her side for thirty years until her death. As we got out of the taxi at the Avenue Kléber I could not help comparing the exterior of the apartment, comparatively new, built early in the twentieth century in the opulent international style found in all European cities, with the history-saturated façade of the Palais-Royal. We went upstairs in the mirrored lift, a candy box that smelled of expensive perfume. Goudeket greeted us at the door. I had not met him before although my husband had published his two books, reminiscences of Colette.

Now he was in his late sixties — Colette would have been close to ninety — but he appeared younger than his age. He was short with a closely-knit vigorous body and the face of a refined pugilist. He had a flat nose and large prominent ears, but his eyes were subtle, the green-brown color of fallen leaves in a summer forest. His voice was soft. He introduced us to his wife and guests, who appeared of one kind, chic, smooth, perfumed; I detected the odor that had permeated the elevator. It was as though Maurice Goudeket had strayed from another world into an exclusive boutique. He was a graceful host, polite to company and deferential to his handsome blonde wife who was about twenty years his junior. Yet he remained self-contained, almost sphinx-like in his remoteness, until a door opened and a baby boy came into the room. Goudeket followed his son with an expression in which the joy of possession and love were mingled with disbelief as before a miracle. "This is Laurent," he said. The child was a miniature of his father, with the same pugilist ears and nose and elfin eyes. Goudeket was saying that because he was so old to be a father for the first time he must make the most of every moment. He could take nothing for granted. He never traveled anymore since he could not be parted from Laurent. He could not afford to lose even one day of his fatherhood. Laurent's nanny came to take him to bed — incongruously, as no amount of English governesses, private tutoring, and pampering could remove the impression that Laurent, like his father, could find his way about without assistance. He had the know-how and grace of a hardy city kitten.

When Laurent had been led away, we moved into the dining room crammed with crystal, china, and flowers.

Goudeket, seated beside me, went on talking as though there had been no interruption. He told me that after Colette's death he had stayed on in their apartment in the Palais-Royal and had become a sort of custodian, a curator of everything she had left behind: her writings, her furniture, her cats, dogs, her neighbors — even the view from her bed into the Palais-Royal garden — until he seemed to hear her voice saying to him that life was to be lived . . .

The conversation around the table was concerned with gambling at Monte Carlo, the "season" at Biarritz, the races at Auteuil and Longchamps. Goudeket remained unfalteringly polite, a dignified outsider replete with an interior life of his own. When he realized how much I admired Colette's books, he talked about them with love and understanding, always modest about his role in their joint life. His was the self-effacement that is related to self-assurance. For Maurice Goudeket the thirty years with Colette were not ended, she lived on as his life principle. The murmur around the table was growing indistinguishable, the sleek, well-dressed guests, blurred. When a bowl of fruit was offered I helped myself to a peach. Before taking my first bite I fondled its rose gold perfection, enjoying the texture of its fuzzy skin like the top of an infant's head and its smell like orchards in the sun. And then I knew that Colette was nearby, the sorceress-interpreter of nature was present, conjured up by her husband's gentle medium-like spell.

Not long ago when I saw Maurice Goudeket I noted that he had aged, not dramatically, but in small ways. Always quiet, his repose now seemed economical, a conservation of his strength. Though still erect, he moved more slowly and his short wiry stature looked diminished. His wife hovered around him, tactfully concerned with his well-being and his wishes. The four of us were driving to a restaurant through a section of Paris that I did not recognize. Streets moving past the windows of the car were without individuality or color, like the setting of an inexpensive film in which, for reasons of budget, the location is some anonymous city and motion and camera angles have substituted for visual interest. I saw no vistas, colonnaded squares, historic monuments, or medieval alleys. The gray buildings flanking the wide avenue were without age or beauty and I felt neither curiosity nor that peculiar gluttony to know Paris more intimately.

At the restaurant we studied the large menus printed in pale purple rococo script, the common writing of gastronomy, like travelers consulting a map on which the route has been inked in by their Michelin guide. While we waited for the *escargots*, we crumbled the hard rolls, unfolded the stiff white napkins and made conversation that was as conventional as these pre-dining gestures. This time Maurice Goudeket did not seem detached. He was as dignified as ever, but the sphinx-like remoteness had vanished. He joined the small talk like someone who has completed a course in a foreign tongue. Always gallant and considerate toward his wife, he now seemed somewhat dependent. They spoke of Laurent, now a schoolboy, their plans for the summer at her house in Biarritz, her hopes to visit the United States, and his reluctance to leave his son. "You know I'm almost eighty now," he said. Colette's name cropped up in the conversation. Maurice Goudeket no longer seemed attentive to that firm voice audible to him alone; his interior life had deserted him. He spoke of Colette with quiet respect. He and my husband discussed royalties and plans for a theatrical production of one of her novels. His wife talked about Colette also, with familiarity and affection, as though referring to a mutual relative, an old aunt recently deceased. As for me, for the first time in Goudeket's company Colette was absent. I felt a twinge of sadness, not for her but for the living, who are compelled to travel through time on a moving belt as, almost unwittingly, they jettison along the way, one by one, the places and the people they had once treasured and re-created in their minds.

CHAPTER IV

The Doctor

THE CREATURES fashioned from romantic love arise all at once, at a glance. They come unannounced and usually spring up when we are looking in another direction. The deepest emotions often elude recapitulation: memory fails, the pain from a serious wound cannot be recalled. But the imagination is no less active with lighter materials. And from first to last, all our creations are subject to change and evolution, so that when we come to the final views, they are scarcely related to the first. It is only after we have arrived at the last chapter that the opening can be written.

This, then, is my completed story of Doctor Walker Buchanan. It came to me on the day I went to view my first grandchild at a New York City hospital. The telephone call from my son, in the early hours, ushered in a new era for all the family. But at that moment, my mind alone registered the event. The appropriate emotions were still dormant and I felt only enormous relief that everyone was well.

A few hours later on Thanksgiving morning, my birthday

as well as my new granddaughter's, my husband and I set out for the hospital. It was one of those clear, cool days the city occasionally presents to its inhabitants. It was especially welcome as the previous day had been tepid, lowering, smog-laden, containing no promise of this brilliant clearing, just as the world had had no trace of this new individual we were about to meet. She was a birthday present to me — on Thanksgiving. In recent years, the holiday had produced neither the ceremonial turkey nor the ragamuffins in their oversized shoes and floppy rags, with their painted vermilion cheeks. Birthday celebrations, like the ragamuffins and the turkey, had been mislaid, and the day had come to signify only the addition of another unwanted year. Now the double holiday had been revived with a new cause for thanksgiving and it was in a spirit of solemn, ritual joy that I approached the hospital.

Once we were inside, my mood struggled to survive the clinical atmosphere: the sight of doctors in white tunics, stretchers, the smell of ether and disinfectant, the soulless voice of the loudspeaker transmitting some urgent, alarming appeal. When we stepped out of the elevator at the maternity floor, the smells and sounds persisted but the sights were more cheerful. Young women in negligées were promenading up and down the corridor like passengers on a ship's deck, snug captives in an incapsulated world for the duration of a short journey.

My husband and I found our daughter-in-law's room and saw her propped against the pillows, looking lovely with her long tawny hair falling over the shoulders of a black Chinese kimono. I was somehow startled that her appearance was much the same as on the previous day, only the great bulge of her belly gone. But then it had always looked extraneous, like an unbecoming article of apparel, now discarded. "Have you seen Laura yet?" she asked with shy pride.

We were directed by a brisk nurse, seemingly unconscious of the drama of new life surrounding her, to the glass of the display window where rows of babies, scraps of almost identical flesh, were exhibited in baskets with their last names on cards for identification. We found ours and admired her neat, round head and tiny features. Her eyes were tightly shut, as though she were not yet ready to face the import of her arrival, and I felt that my intense gaze must surely waken her. But as I continued to peer into the hospital nursery, the past suddenly engulfed me and I found myself looking at the same heart-shaped face and perfect miniature hands; instead, they belonged to my newborn son, now separated from me by twenty-three years — and, then, by an identical glass partition and by the overbearing, stocky presence of Doctor Walker Buchanan . . .

The walls of Doctor Buchanan's waiting room were crowded with photographs of infants he had brought into the world. Out of assorted frames they smiled, in all stages of growth — newborn and naked, or dressed in frilly pinafores, posed on summer lawns in Southampton or Greenwich. But, oddly, when one reached Doctor Buchanan's office, the inner sanctum where he sat, solidly, complacently enthroned behind his expensive desk, the topic of babies seemed farthest from his mind. Childless himself, women, not their progeny, interested him. He had a broad, ruddy, sun-tanned face, a blunt, fat nose, and wide-set brown eyes which reflected his good opinion of himself and his connoisseur's pleasure in the pretty young creatures who were his patients. Their level of pulchritude was high, for an older woman rarely strayed onto the premises. Born in Texas, he was an ardent Anglophile. He had a small well-trimmed mustache and always wore brown tweed suits made for him in London. At our first meeting, when I received the overwhelming information that I was to have a child, I was surprised that he seemed to be concerned solely with the virtues of Great Britain as contrasted with the vices of the Soviet Union. But as the months passed, surprise evaporated, and like everyone else I accepted the endless lectures. Sitting in the waiting room, as the minutes piled up, one could reproduce the monologue in a southern accent going on behind the closed door of Doctor Buchanan's office. ". . . I have to hand it to the English. They're all that's left of our civilization — first in science, war skills, and governmental know-how — but those Reds — dreadful microbes — we should blast them off the face of the earth. It's beyond me the way the United States panders to them! . . ." The year was 1943.

While Doctor Buchanan held forth, his docile patient might be thinking about her morning sickness and its possible cure, or wondering about the date of her delivery, but she knew better than to interrupt him. Nor did she protest the endless waiting before she could be admitted to the doctor's presence. After she had leafed through all the magazines and re-examined each baby portrait the door of the office would open, and Doctor Buchanan would step, with deliberation, into the waiting room. His small eyes twinkling at the sight of his pretty subjects, he would announce simply, "Next." Then, tossing back her mane of glossy hair and balancing, not ungracefully, her loaded stomach, in strict order of arrival a patient would rise and disappear inside.

The office routine was regulated by an efficient, antiseptic nurse, Miss Fleetman, assisted by a maid in uniform with an embroidered organdy apron, like a stage domestic. Miss Fleetman was middle-aged but trim, with sharp features and gray-blond hair pulled back severely into a black bow. When one was helplessly caught on the examining table, Miss Fleetman was fond of telling pointless jokes, and if the response was deficient she did not hesitate to register her scorn. She danced tireless attendance on Doctor Buchanan, and it was obvious that, whatever her own neglected private life might be, she gloried in her role of handmaiden, passing him his rubber gloves and instruments with the ceremoniousness of Hebe, the cup-bearer of Greek mythology. From February to November, I appeared punctually for my appointments with Doctor Buchanan, who seemed less a man than a part of nature, like the steady succession of weeks, months, and seasons.

I felt as though this state of things might continue indefinitely, but one November night it came to an end. The baby announced himself. We arrived at the hospital and were met there by Doctor Buchanan. The encounter reduced my husband and me to vague unrealities. Only my galvanized insides and the bulky person of the doctor, calm as ever, still wearing a brown tweed suit but silent, for once, on the subject of "Commies," had importance. "I'll be back in the morning," he said, "there won't be any real action before then."

After Doctor Buchanan and my husband had gone, I lay rigid and frightened, listening to the rattle of the radiators. They were like old arteries, reluctantly pumping heat through the hospital. At intervals, during the night, the loudspeaker

called for this or that, but, because of the shortage of nurses
due to the war, I saw no human face.

I opened my eyes to a new dim world. Somewhere far off,
seen through the wrong end of a telescope, a lamp shed its
pale glow. It cast squares of light and shade on walls and
ceiling, and like an ancient writing these shapes spelled a
malevolent meaning to me. I turned my head to the window,
but the curtains were drawn and the sleeping window could
show me no accustomed landmark, no piece of sky with star
or sun to tell the time of day.

Then suddenly the whistle of a riverboat broke the padded
stillness; nostalgic and searching, it brought a chain of returning memories. I had stood on a ship's deck, high above
the dock, and felt a great engine come to life beneath my
feet. I had seen a chasm widening between me and the
tiny blank faces below. Flowered hats blurred into a mosaic
of color, shouted goodbyes merged into meaningless sound.
Without relenting, the ship severed us from the unresisting
land. Then the riverboat whistled, speaking of new places
and unhinted experience. River whistles meant partings and
promises — and pain — a sharp thrust of pain that had pinned
me through the groin, deep into the bed, and then floated
me up to heights without foundation. Outside, the riverboat shrilled in unheeding syncopation to the steady rhythm
of pain.

Then a corridor of oblivion had led to this small place of
oblique light and quiet where I now lay. I waited eagerly
for the next assault, a familiar enemy in this strangeness. Why
do I feel nothing but numbness? When does the next pain
begin? I heard a starched rustle and then a figure emerged,

white and shapeless, topped by a tiny clown's cap of puffed organdy — a meaningless dweller in this senseless planet.

"I'm Miss Coates. You have a fine son."

Unbelieving, I clung to the memory of pain, ebbing and returning in cruel regularity. There was a clatter of wheels, the opening of a door, and again the rustle that announced Miss Coates, accompanied by a faint smell of lavender talcum. The night light over my head was bright as, dazed and dizzy, I peered into a basket where the baby lay, minuscule, greedily abandoned to sleep. His smooth legs thrust out from the diaper like pink-tan drumsticks from a white napkin. Automatically, I counted ten toes and ten fingers, each topped by a microscopic nail. With a self-righteous sigh of exhaustion, I dropped back into darkness. The last thing I heard as deep sleep overtook me was the dwindling rattle of the baby cart disappearing down the hall, like a sound of a solitary milk wagon from my childhood following its route through dawn-lonely city streets.

The metallic November sun was everywhere in my room. Outside it glinted on the river with intolerable brightness, uncovering the island institution buildings and the opposite shore in sharp, primitive detail. My window could not shut out the cold forsaken sound of the wind, but it sheltered me from the blast. The room was as gently warm as a spring day, and I lay in a cocoon of comfort and dependence. Flowers sprouted on all sides, in every inch of space, like a carelessly planted garden. On either end of the bureau, two noble bouquets of chrysanthemums stood sentinel in flat-footed hospital vases. Between these, roses bloomed in unseasonal profusion; tight pink buds, full-blown yellow, sunlit ones, deep valentine red ones. My bedside table had been cleared to make space for a potted bush on which one perfect white gardenia grew alone among glossy green leaves. Across the room a fleshy, purple orchid stood in a glass test tube, and two empty porcelain baby shoes denoted the passage of time. The days were punctuated by the arrival of new florist boxes and the departure of fading bouquets, and by regular visits from my son and Doctor Walker Buchanan.

That first morning, I found Doctor Buchanan, a massive tower, standing over me. His fingers on my lax wrist were strong and cool from the wintry day outside. In my weakness, I could hear my own voice as from a distance, babbling my gratitude to him for the miracle of delivering a baby. It seemed his miracle — not mine — for he had been there throughout, while I had been reduced to that faraway black world, unassisting, unknowing. I could dimly remember him under the kleig lights, in a white coat and cap, his brown eyes intent above a mask, his voice authoritative, his hands unhesitating. He could not have been the same man I visited in the office, who sat casually behind a desk in a brown tweed suit. He had issued the command for a hypodermic to put me out of pain. Though I tried to protest — I could bear more — I struggled against my expendability in vain, and darkness overtook me.

After the delivery, I was to remember each of his calls with bright separateness. I relived the time he arrived unexpectedly in the afternoon as I lay uncomfortably tense and wakeful in blind obedience to the inflexible hospital etiquette of "naps."

"How is the prize guinea pig today?"

"Fine," I lied, feeling each nerve jump individually. There

was a tacit code of behavior between us, enthusiastic admiration on my part, unsurprised acceptance on his. Any complaint would mar my self-imposed act of grateful well-being.

"Good. This performance, you know, has been wholly satisfactory."

"Whose performance?" I asked.

"Yours and mine," Doctor Buchanan answered.

We both smiled. When he had gone I felt the muscles of my legs and back unknot with mesmerized ease, and as I fell asleep I remembered the words "yours and mine," and hugged them to me as a new and intimate truth.

There was another day when his visit came as I was returning to bed, with weak relief, after my first time up. I had walked down the hall to the nursery to look at my son through the glass partition. I had noted his domed forehead with a fringe of light hair, his neatly marked brows, his eyes, creased in sleep, but he was just the representation of a baby. When he was brought to me, his eyes were usually open in a rage of hunger. But this was only at stated minutes, with a nurse standing by, ready to snatch him back to his communal home. I made the ascent into the high bed with humiliating slowness. Like a stimulant, Doctor Buchanan's vitality was necessary to my weakness, which he took for granted and transformed into a feeling of gracious feminine dependence.

Now, on this morning, I sat propped high in bed in the sunny room, thinking of past visits and waiting for the approaching one with admitted impatience. A book lay open on my lap, its pages never turned. In the fake Regency mirror over the bureau, directly facing the bed, my image had confronted me with tactless insistence all these days.

This morning, though, I was not displeased by what I saw. In the coarse white hospital nightgown, with my dark hair falling in a straight, heavy fold to my shoulders, I looked like a clinical medieval acolyte. I had repeatedly refused the nurse's attempts to make me wear the pale blue bed jacket, curly with ruffles and lace, that hung unused in the closet. The austerity of the hospital nightgown had suited my mood, symbolizing my removal from the everyday world to these cloistered confines.

I could hear the nurse's familiar walk, her rubber heels squeaking on the linoleum floor of the hall. Then her voice broke hoarsely into song, its words reaching me with gusty pathos: "Lay that pistol down, babe, lay that pistol down, pistol-packin' mama, lay that pistol down . . ."

Her head appeared around the screen at the door. "Doctor Buchanan is on his way up. Is there anything you need before I go down for my lunch?"

I had learned that this type of question required no response. I felt my heart beating thickly. Then the elevator groaned open, the nurse's head disappeared, and Doctor Buchanan stood in the room. I felt his presence more than I saw it.

I waited for him to sit down as usual in the expectant, spindly chair that always creaked precariously beneath his unselfconscious weight. Instead, he walked directly to the gardenia plant, and with deft fingers plucked the flower and placed it in his buttonhole. "You won't miss this?"

I don't remember my answer, because just then I noticed the faint unmistakable smell of ether on Doctor Buchanan's fingers as he plucked the gardenia. Like the proverbial tell-tale perfume on a husband's clothes, it choked me with angry possessiveness.

"I just ran into Doctor Howard Hooton in the hall. Do you know him?"

"By sight, only," I answered, absently.

"It's hard to believe that that poor man is five years younger than I am. He looks a hundred."

In those days I rarely thought of age in connection with Doctor Buchanan. His store of strength and Jovian self-confidence belonged to neither youth nor age but simply to a state of being peculiar to him.

"The trouble with him," Doctor Buchanan went on, "is that he worries too much. I told him so."

I had a vision of the small, sere Doctor Hooton being blown down the hall on the momentum of Doctor Buchanan's hearty advice like a dry autum leaf in a bluff wind.

"I never worry about my patients," the doctor stated confidentially. "I always feel they'll come out all right. And somehow, they always do."

As he talked, he stood in front of the window, almost filling it with his square outline. But now the steel prow of a merchant ship appeared within the limited frame of my vision. I caught sight of its rusty side, used and ugly with demands of war. Then it was hidden from sight by Doctor Buchanan's broad back. I had a guilty feeling of having escaped from the world so that not even a disturbing sight could remind me of what lay outside.

"Will you have a cigarette?" Doctor Buchanan produced a crumpled package. I took one; it felt warm from the inside of his pocket.

He sat down, tilting the chair to a dangerous angle. The

cigarette was cupped in his hand, the smoke spiraling toward his wrist, where the dark hair showed beneath an immaculate white cuff.

"I'd be a great advertisement for cigarettes," Doctor Buchanan announced with pride. "I haven't stopped smoking since I was ten."

"It didn't stunt your growth, at any rate," I said.

He looked pleased. "I can remember my first puff. It was one of those stifling Texas summer days —"

This would be a long anecdote. I sank back on my pillows, luxuriating in their softness and in the masculine, even depth of Doctor Buchanan's voice.

"It was too hot to play baseball," he continued, "so I decided to carry out a project I'd had in mind for some time. I retreated to the privacy of the tool shed in the back yard with a smuggled box of cigarettes. My father found me there, with a cigarette in my mouth, and he beat me so hard I can still feel it."

"How terrible," I said, smarting with sympathetic indignation.

"Not so terrible," he countered. "As my father hit me, he explained that this was not so much a punishment as an illustration of what life was like. He and I were never good friends, but I thank him for that lesson."

"What did you learn?"

"I learned from that one lesson to be invulnerable and independent and I've been that ever since," Doctor Buchanan replied, with the bluntness of a man who is too honest to pretend that he is not satisfied with himself.

He consulted his pocket watch (a gift from a grateful patient, I imagined), and rose to his feet without haste. "I had no idea it was so late," he said. He was standing at the foot of my bed. "You have been a darn good patient. I am going to miss these visits, fellow," he added.

I had heard the casually endearing word before, but today it sounded special. His eyes met mine and from their still darkness a powerful current shot through me. I turned away as Doctor Buchanan continued with jocose unawareness, "Today is Monday. If all goes well, I guess I'll have to release you from jail on Thursday."

The elevator clanged again, so I knew he had gone. Monday to Thursday, and then this strange new world would end as suddenly as it had begun. It was five o'clock, the gray hour at the hospital. The sun had left the river, which was now veiled in gray mist. My room was in semi-darkness, the lights not yet switched on. I could hear voices, near and distant, saying goodbye in the forced, cheerful tones used by visitors in a hospital. The radiators rattled.

I turned on the radio next to my bed, and a hoarse voice boomed, "Lay that pistol down, babe — " Suddenly I felt a flood of warm excitement, a spicy sense of expectation. As the singer roared his last refrain, I said to myself, "Monday to Thursday, that's three days, and three days can seem an eternity in a hospital."

I sat on the edge of the bed; the room had been cleared of my belongings and showed no trace of occupancy. A packed suitcase stood waiting at the door. The bed had been stripped and the mattress was revealed in naked indeceny. Tables and bureau were bare, but one congratulatory picture card was still stuck in the mirror with lonely bravura.

My last morning had dragged by. I had tried to recapture

and cling to the solace of familiar sights and feelings, turned coldly elusive and unfamiliar, now that departure was imminent. The very walls seemed to push me outside with the rude impatience of a hotel room about to be vacated. Doctor Buchanan's last call had slipped by, an unaccented beat in a minor melody. With bland habit he dismissed my case. "We'll have to give you your diploma now. But if you should need me, you know where to reach me."

"I'll be all right," I said without interest.

"You'll be all right if you don't overdo," Doctor Buchanan admonished. "Rest every afternoon. Don't be too gay — "

Through the half open door I heard a man's footfall approaching with brisk steps. It might be my husband. I expected him soon, to take me and the baby home. I listened attentively but the footsteps passed my room and I heard an imperious knock on the door next to mine.

Doctor Buchanan closed his bag with a final snap. "You don't belong here any longer, I can see that," he said. "You're not even listening to your doctor's last words of wisdom." He picked up the bag, grasped my hand with false heartiness, and was gone.

I waited, feeling strangely small and alone, suspended between two worlds. Responsibility was new, a numb limb that came to life achingly as I reluctantly prepared to take a first step.

Now the baby lay beside me on the bed. He was dressed for departure in a blue bunting that revealed his face, round and rosy as a summer cloud. For no reason, he began to cry, loud and furious. His face colored a sudden deep red, leaving only his nose a small white raspberry. Bewildered and loving, I picked him up. With sensual pleasure I felt his heavy warm weight in my arms, and for the first time he seemed completely mine. Unexpectedly, a river boat whistled. "Parting and promise, parting and promise," it insisted, with piercing repetition. I slid from the bed, and with the baby in my arms, I stood ready and eager for the door to open.

During the following years, occasional office visits to Doctor Buchanan were in order. He held sway again behind his desk. But my other self, austerely garbed in a hospital gown, had departed like a ghost. Out of a kind of mistaken loyalty, I did dress with unusual care in preparation for these rare appointments, only to be bored by the resumed lectures. Now that the war was over, Doctor Buchanan had an I-told-you-so attitude about the Russians and the Cold War. It was a situation he could easily have averted had he not been so busy, moving surely but without haste between office and delivery room. When his telephone buzzed he would pick up the receiver without removing his calm gaze from my face. Playing with the gold watch chain that spanned his ample stomach like a delicate suspension bridge, he would say into the telephone, "Take it easy, fellow. I'll be there soon. Time the intervals between pains, nothin' is going to happen to you." I felt at such times that I was eavesdropping indecently. Sometimes, Doctor Buchanan would intersperse his predictions on international affairs with boasts about his week-end golf scores at Southampton. Suppressing a polite yawn, I would listen to his low, monotonous voice, trying to remember how it could take command at a moment's notice. But it was all as impersonal as before the birth and the baby was never mentioned except by Miss Fleetman, who would inquire about him before starting off on one of her interminable jokes. True, my son's photograph had joined the parade on the crowded walls of the waiting room. I marveled that space had been available, and my eyes, as though magnetized, were drawn to his face away from all the rest. Once Doctor Buchanan stopped and asked abruptly, "Isn't it about time for another baby?" The question startled me and caused a mild embarrassment. It sounded like the perfunctory proposition of a somewhat jaded roué.

Years after, looking at my granddaughter through the glass partition of the hospital nursery, these successive images of Doctor Buchanan returned to me. He was now dead. As he had grown older, his practice had thinned; he had moved from his former office with the spacious waiting room, with its old-fashioned, home-like sofas, chairs, tables, and lamps, and had relocated in the impersonal premises of a medical building. The baby photographs had disappeared along with the maid in the embroidered organdy apron. But Miss Fleetman still bustled about these new quarters as though there had been no change, still wearing a black velvet bow, still indulging in pointless jokes, still worshipping the doctor. He had aged without any appreciable physical alteration, only his deliberate step had grown somewhat slower and his small mustache more grizzled.

The last visit had begun like all the rest and I had listened to the same old diatribe on the Russians. It was less lengthy a process these days, because the waiting room was cramped, in spite of the fact that the patients were fewer. The young girls with their swollen bellies balanced over their pretty legs had migrated elsewhere. The clientele consisted mainly of aging women wearing too much jewelry.

After Doctor Buchanan had examined me, he stated — in

a voice so matter of fact I thought I had misunderstood him —
that I had a condition necessitating immediate hysterectomy.
When his meaning finally penetrated, I protested my good
health and the risk of surgery.

"Why such a fuss?" he said. "With me, the operation is
nothin' at all. I have a special system for tying off the arteries
that all my colleagues envy. I could do it in my sleep, and
you'd be safer than with the other guys."

His Jovian confidence had become a threat. "Miss Fleetman," he was calling in a testy voice, pressing the bell on
his desk. She materialized in the doorway. "Reserve a room
at the hospital for tomorrow," he said.

As though under attack, I started to back out. My ears
were humming in noisy concert with the air conditioner, and
it was difficult to breathe. I felt that space had shrunk and
that Doctor Buchanan, abnormally large, was blocking my
exit. I still protested. Looking up from a prescription pad
on which he had been scribbling, the doctor shot me one
of his long, level looks. "What do you need that piece of
meat for, anyhow?" he asked.

I fled, with the guilty intention of consulting a new doctor
— who did in fact give me the welcome verdict that no operation was required. I never saw Doctor Buchanan again, nor
did he telephone to inquire about my defection. Afterwards,
I gave him no thought until the morning I read his obituary
in the newspaper. He was no different from all the other
dead with vaguely familiar names.

But now, on this day of my granddaughter's birth, Doctor
Buchanan returned to me, and that final meeting that had
been so alarmingly meaningless became the last pitiful chapter in my memory of him. Here was the aging doctor, re-

tired from obstetrics but still clinging to surgery. I saw him maddened by his dwindling practice, deprived of that intoxicating, mesmeric dominance that could take charge with such assurance — that could even rob his patients of the experience of childbirth. This power was slipping away, and with all his might he yearned for it — "Reserve a room at the hospital for tomorrow." With hallucinated clarity, I saw an old general with a butcher's face, brandishing an imaginary blade, lusting to enter a combat that was his no longer.

CHAPTER V

The Culture Professionals

THE MEANING of "culture professional" is not to be found in the dictionary. By my definition it is someone who promotes the arts, which, in turn, enhance his own status. Money, talent, charm, brains, political or social power may be used for this purpose. Although the culture professional is a manipulator, he is also frequently a benefactor. For me, Stanley Young and his wife, the writer Nancy Wilson Ross, were archetypes out of my past, encountered along the circuitous route of accident and circumstance.

What is left for me to remember of the war years? Scraps of souvenirs glimpsed between the piled bricks of day-to-day living: there was the sight of the rusty ship, almost hidden behind the broad back of Doctor Buchanan; newspaper headlines that implanted in my consciousness such heretofore unknown places as Iwo Jima, St. Lô, Guadalcanal, Anzio Beachhead; the familiar, sedative voice of the newscaster over the radio, making household heroes out of the names of MacArthur, Patton, Stilwell — resplendent for their brief span, like Fourth of July rockets, before subsiding into past glory. Today I am returned in time, when I hear the siren proclaiming a peaceful noon. It is the same sound that used to announce air raid practice — a warning, followed by an all-clear, conjuring up images of gas masks like nightmare elephant trunks, and shelters under city streets ready to offer claustrophobic hospitality to the beleaguered.

There was the summer weekend my husband (on leave from the Navy) and I spent at his family's fishing retreat in upstate New York. The murmurous river was calm, and so were the mingled smells of dry pine and hay and the sight of the trim white house with its red shutters. But the small clearing in the woods and the heavy heat were oppressive, and, far off, the war was continuing its relentless way. I sat in a garden rocker on the flagstone terrace above the river, surrounded by pots of geraniums under a candy-striped awning. I was enjoying the sight of my husband in tall waders, his fishing rod over his shoulder, his creel filled with trout, climbing nimbly up the embankment toward the terrace. At the edge of the clearing, Mr. Ertz, the farmer, was plodding back and forth from the barn. Like the hot summer weather, there was in Mr. Ertz a submerged threat. His healthful outdoor existence was marred by the horror stories he delighted in telling. He would often pause in his chores when he spied me, idle, on the terrace. "Just heard that the Maples' cow gave birth to a three-legged calf," or "Awful motor accident down Bearsville way, car wrecked, everyone killed." His thin-lipped, colorless face would remain expressionless, but as he picked up his pitchfork or pail he seemed to derive new energy from the discharge of another calamity. I watched him walking steadily along the path and as he drew near I felt the latest news, like an ugly herald, going before him. I pretended to be reading but it was useless; he was standing close to me, pushing his battered felt hat back from his perspiring forehead, holding his silence a moment longer for effectiveness. Then, "Heard over the radio, we just exploded an atom bomb in Japan — destroyed a whole city and everyone in it. No one has ever seen the like — ." The three-legged calf, the automobile crash, the atom bomb — and Mr. Ertz moving down the road, his burdens made lighter by the delivery of another disaster — the summer sky darkening and the rumble of thunder announcing the approach of a storm.

In war as in peace we are, for the most part, selfish and egocentric, and the climax of the war for me was my husband's tour of duty in the Pacific. As the day of departure drew near, threatened, he became once again the dazzling stranger I had married five years earlier. He appeared more handsome in his blue and gold ensign's uniform, more desirable, never to be taken for granted. When he had gone, flying toward some distant island — tropical, evil, erupting — I felt abandoned, perched high in our apartment, unhomelike in its loneliness, with my infant son, a responsibility grown heavy because I was alone. The nursery was sunlit, overlooking the reservoir in Central Park where the changing light recorded the hours of the day. One afternoon, a friend came to see the baby with her husband, a lieutenant who had just received orders for combat in Europe. I can still recreate the scene: the bright nursery, papered yellow and white with a light-hearted frieze parading around the walls, the baby in his crib and the visitors bending over it, admiring him. Is it hindsight that makes me see the young lieutenant, rosy cheeked, curly haired, in his new infantry khaki, within a bower of light more brilliant than the sunny nursery? It may be — because he never returned. He was killed in the Normandy Invasion, and he has left behind in my memory that last picture of him by the side of the crib, his scrubbed, snub-nosed face illumined like an image in a medieval book of saints.

I can recall little of those long weeks of separation. Occasionally, a letter from my husband reached me. Although I would read it many times, the words were disappointingly inadequate, but the thin air-mail paper he had touched had value. I lived with a constant sensation of helpless anxiety, the threat of falling victim to the churning public events. I tried to drown fear in small household duties. But when I looked at my son, my heart would often lurch heavily, for he too might be a sacrifice. And it seemed to me that childhood was pathetic, even more vulnerable, ignorant, and hopeful than the adult world. I watched the baby taking his first steps and my happiness was feigned. I wanted my husband to share the moment, to guide the teetering attempts around the chintz cliffs of the sofa and to right the tumbles on the wide terrain of the living-room carpet. And all the while I had the feeling that it was I who would never learn to walk alone.

One morning, as though directed by radar, I made the discovery of writing. Here was the antidote to anxiety; a world that I could order, an escape from the treacheries of the day. With the aid of memory, I was empowered to resurrect a sleeping past and bathe it in the varied colors of my own imagination.

I wrote a story and it was quickly finished, and then

quickly forgotten with my husband's return. I remember the airport filled with men in uniform. The arrival of the awaited plane cut my breath with joy and awe. I was caught in the toils of the giant supernatural bird, blinded by its dazzling wings and deafened by its uproar. When it settled to the ground, I strained to identify my husband among the small humans that were being disgorged from a hole in its side. Where had they been? What had they seen? At last I spotted him, his uniform creased, his black hair rumpled, his sun-burned face looking tired. And I noticed that, oddly, he was wearing the scuffed house slippers I used to know next to the bed. Later, I learned that this was because he had cut his foot on a coral reef. But at the moment of arrival it seemed an intimate, loving gesture, a reassurance that our separation and the intervention of so many miles, alien places, and experiences had not, after all, made him a foreigner to home and to me.

The war in the Pacific ended as I was listening to the news one night on a summer porch. The announcer's voice was accompanied by insect wings making their tiny barrage against the screens and by a chorus of tree toads croaking all around us in their dusky green hideaways. The European war was over for me with even less emphasis, and with indecent haste its memory dropped away. Only the sight of a young paraplegic in a wheelchair, the upper part of his body aglow with animal health and strength, his unrelated legs wasted and useless, was a reminder — or meeting a wife and mother for whom family life was not resumed. I tried to hold on to the exhilaration of reunion and the relief of security, but they too slipped by in the midst of my treasuring.

One day when I was clearing out my desk drawer, I came

across the story; it seemed to me, now, in another life, written by a different person. It lay valueless among old invitations, checkbooks, stamps, and discarded snapshots of the baby. Yet with a kind of stubborn loyalty to the fulfillment it had once afforded me, before burying it with the rest of the trash, I gave it to my husband to read. "It's good," he said. "I'd like to show it to Stanley Young. He's one of the best younger editors in town, and a poet himself, besides." In this roundabout way, Stanley Young and his wife Nancy were introduced into my life. And I entered theirs through the stone gate posts that led into the flourishing acres of The Orchards, the Long Island estate of the Wentworth family, that provided the Youngs their fastness against the world.

I suppose that Stanley had pronounced his approval of my writing before that first visit, because my entry at The Orchards is accompanied in memory by a new awareness of accomplishment that radiated through me with the stimulating warmth of fine spirits. And as I stepped across the threshold, though uncertain, I felt at once the embrace of this new world, as the most insignificant choir boy partakes of the pageantry of the church, and, though far below him, is yet germane to the ultramundane person of the priest. At The Orchards, a priest and priestess officiated jointly. The Youngs lived in the gatehouse to the estate. It was ordinary enough from the outside, made of gray shingles with a covered veranda leading to the door. But once within one was enveloped by the strong odor of incense, and it was so dusky that only a shaft of bland Long Island sun lit up, here and there, a strip of Chinese calligraphy hanging on a wall, an enigmatic stone figurine of the god Shiva, or a single rosy tinted spray of orange blossoms that seemed as weighted with meaning as the Cross.

Stanley and his wife greeted us. He was a tall, springy man, with a shock of tawny hair and a virile, ruddy pioneer's face. Only his eyes, of an intense blue like Sterno flame, hinted at a connection with the spiritual world. His words might be bluff but his glance seemed to be saying, "You and I are special — we do not belong to the world of Philistines." He was dressed in a turtleneck sweater and tweedy jacket with patched elbows, more indigenous to the paddocks, tennis courts, and game rooms of The Orchards than the modified sari and long ropes of Oriental beads worn by his wife. She, too, had a mane of tawny hair and, although she was short, hardly reaching her husband's shoulder, she gave the impression of greater strength. She was beautiful, with large, dreamy amber eyes, so wide-set that they seemed to be looking in two opposite directions at once, toward the disparate cultures of East and West whose threads she blended on her person and in her home like strands woven from an invisible loom. At the time of our first meeting, Nancy and Stanley were newly married, but they seemed already to be a team guarding in mutual understanding the sacred premises of the arts and admitting only the select through the doors of the temple.

The visits to The Orchards merge in my memory because of their sameness, differentiated only by the revolving seasons. In the winter the Youngs and their guests remained indoors, ensconced in the Bauhaus chairs and sofas. These chunky free-form pieces had a dated look, like popular flappers grown ungainly in their middle years but still considered audacious. Nancy had studied in Germany at the Bauhaus when she was young and her furniture was the legacy of those times. On the walls were Oriental paintings, attesting to her enthusiasm for Zen. She was the author of several novels that subtly combine her American roots with an Oriental cast of mind. And her learned books on Zen have the kind of intensity that only an outsider can bring to an alien culture. She presided among her collections and her guests with a connoisseur's pleasure in their worth. The guests were of various ages and belonged to all the arts. They came and went, but a hard core of wealthy Long Island and New York socialites remained. Always present was Priscilla, born a Wentworth and married to a Yugoslav journalist. An actress, she was the daughter of the owner of The Orchards, and in her quiet way a rebel, having refused to be presented to Long Island society. She preferred the world of the theater and the Youngs gave enthusiastic support to this preference. She dressed in sandals from Greenwich Village and dirndls from Austria, and with her flaming hair, proud bones, and white face she reminded me of a smoldering Hester Prynne. Stanley would sit casually, boyishly at her feet or at mine. But his attitude was never subservient; rather, it was masterful, combining the omniscience of a priest or guru with the natural flirtatiousness of an attractive male in the presence of a young and admiring female. "Are you working?" he would ask, and his Sterno-flame-blue eyes would bore into mine as though reading there the record of my many derelictions. I felt that he saw and disapproved of my walks in Central Park with my son in his baby carriage, the parties I attended, the weekends at our country home — all of my conjugal life. These were my sins — and with his long legs folded tailorwise, his hair becomingly tousled, his ruddy plowman's face turned up to mine, Stanley Young played father-confessor, drawing out my transgressions and forgiving them simultaneously. "Oh, the world is too much with us," he would say, "we must flee, we must shut ourselves away; for the artist, work is the only salvation."

I was by nature an outsider to this monastic utopia recommended by the Youngs, but their inclusion of me was flattering and stimulating. I would watch Nancy poring over a Japanese print, exclaiming at its frugal beauty and explaining its occult meaning. Sometimes she would look up with a sigh and softly take up her husband's refrain but with a greater emphasis, "Yes, the world is monstrous. It is our duty to protect ourselves." And at The Orchards I always did feel protected but exalted too, with that amorphous thrill experienced during the moment of silence before a great performer strikes the opening notes on the keyboard.

When the weather was fair, the Youngs would stroll with their guests over the spacious grounds of The Orchards. Although they were only tenants, living rent-free in the Gate-house, they seemed to be the true lords of the place. At the end of winter we would find the snow melting in porous patches beneath the great old trees that, in summer, had cast patterns of leaf-dancing shade over the mowed and watered lawns. The swimming pool was encircled by a ring of Buddhas which, even transported from so far away, looked at home at The Orchards. However, their sleepy stone faces above the clear aquamarine of the water seemed to be issuing a warning from the ancient, static wisdom of the East to the heedless, enterprising West that their jewels were dearly bought and transient. As we walked around the flower gardens, the orchards, the tennis courts, and the paddocks,

Stanley would bend down to pick up an early autumn apple from the russet and green carpet beneath the bountiful trees. "Still sour," he would say after one bite, and hurl it with athletic speed toward the invisible horizon of the acreage. Or Nancy would pluck a single white rose from a formal bed. "It's too lovely! A perfect creation," she would murmur in prayerful contemplation. It was hard for me to believe that the Youngs had not always been part of the place, that he had sprung from Indiana's parched Corn Belt, that she had begun life in the Northwest in Olympia, Washington. Perhaps it was from there that she had first directed her wide and brooding gaze towards the mysteries of the Orient.

Sometimes we would visit the main house, a conventional Georgian mansion which, after the war, when we were introduced to it, was inhabited by Austin, the youngest Wentworth, and his pretty wife Melissa, with their brood of children. Austin's sister Priscilla would spend the weekends there with her family when she was not detained by a theater engagement. The beauty of Priscilla and Melissa ("Prissy" and "Missy," to the Youngs) was as romantic as the heirloom portraits of bygone wives and mothers of the family adorning the walls of the house. Priscilla's and Melissa's shining hair and correct features were as lovely as the Lowestoft china, Chippendale furniture, mirror brasses, and artful bouquets that surrounded them. And they were as well cared for. But Priscilla was robust and blooming, while Melissa was delicate, bedridden at this time with a touch of tuberculosis contracted when she had been a nurse's aide during the war. Her lingering illness was a reminder of the harsher war days, now quickly disappearing from our memories like the patches of melting snow under the trees outside. Melissa

Wentworth would be sitting up in her high four-poster bed when her five children would be brought to her by an English nanny and her subordinate nursemaids. Melissa would languidly pass their beauty in review, one by one, but at the entrance of the Youngs her face would light up with admiration and trust.

"Look, Missy, I have brought you this perfect rose," Nancy would say, offering the bloom as though it were her own creation.

Nancy's interest would frequently be diverted to the nanny, her apprentices, and their charges and she was on intimate terms with all the Wentworth servants, calling each one by name. She deeply savored the Old World regime of the big house, and I imagined that her vision repainted the scene in the delectable colors of a Fragonard, a far cry from the abstractions and the Chinese calligraphy at the Gatehouse, but in contrast perhaps all the more alluring — for everything is enjoyed as a relief from something else. And I was also certain that all this was raw material for the Youngs, eventually to be transformed in the expression of their own work. That Stanley and Nancy were artists the Wentworths never forgot either. And like the Medicis before them, their generosity was amply rewarded by the presence in their midst of these birds of rare plumage.

I remember especially one hot summer evening in the Youngs' living room. The last few days had produced one of those records noted by the weather bureau with a kind of fatalistic pride — the mercury hovering close to one hundred degrees, the nights bringing no relief but the cessation of the sun, all the more suffocating, like being buried alive in a dark hole. Nothing stirred outdoors; the guests sat in an expectant circle on the Bauhaus furniture, for Stanley was about to read his long poem in progress: *America, my America.* I can recall some of the faces. Timothy was the rebel scion of a conventional, wealthy Boston family, who lived most of the time in a pink villa on the Riviera, endlessly writing the memoirs of his homosexual expatriation. Elsie and Charles Johnson — were there — she had been Nancy's classmate out west. A chirping, elfin woman, interested in textile designing, she had married, moved from Greenwich Village to Sutton Place, and dutifully produced an heir, and I felt that Nancy considered her a defector to the Philistines. The Johnsons, however, were usually included in these gatherings. Then there was the usual assortment of aspiring young writers for whom Stanley, in his role of editor, was guardian and inspiration.

I observed him closely as he glanced through his manuscript before starting to read. As usual, he was sitting on the floor as though taking part in an undergraduate get-together. There was something unusually attractive about his virility and plowman's handsomeness, especially when one knew that it was the outer covering for the soul of a poet. He reminded me of the prince in the fairy tales who had been bewitched into the body of a bear.

"Shall I begin?" he asked, looking with pleasure around his circle.

I do not remember much about *America, my America,* but I can still hear Stanley's rich voice with its trace of midwestern pronunciation, reading on and on, and feel the wicked heat that locked us all in feverish quarantine. And I can still see Nancy spread out on a sofa, dressed in diaphanous Indian gauze of turquoise and gold. The robe encased her body ceremoniously without seeming to touch it, like the tent of a rajah. As her husband read his poem, a few tears trickled from her large eyes, as though their amber were slowly melting from the heat outside and the fire of her emotions within.

I was stirred by the familiar feeling I so often had in the company of the Youngs. It was a combination of my admiration for them and their way of life and the faint stirrings of unrealized possibilities in myself, like an adolescent's first awareness of physical love, a future experience he promises himself, something at once sweetly personal and grandly universal. From far off, I realized that Stanley had stopped reading. Everyone was silent. Then, Nancy, wiping the remaining tears from her eyes, exclaimed, "Can you believe that this man is still a white-collar worker? How I have implored him to leave publishing! It is my mission to see that he shuts the door on the world, once and for all, in order to write, write, write — ."

Stanley did in fact retire from publishing, and his charm has been employed instead on the boards of art councils and foundations. He travels around the country disseminating culture and his still boyish resilient personality. I do not know whether he has ever found the time to complete *America, my America*. Nancy has grown more involved with Eastern philosophy, writing books about it and lecturing. After each trip to the Orient she returns still more adorned with Indian, Japanese, and Thai silks and jewelry, more inwardly withdrawn than ever from the "monstrous" world we all live in. She is still lovely but has grown stouter, and her amber eyes have a hooded look more disillusioned now than dreamy. She reminds me of an ageless owl sagely observing the twitterings and flutterings of the other birds in the forest, more frivolous and less knowing than she. "The group" has been dispersed: Priscilla, divorced and moved to San Francisco, the young Austin Wentworths and their children are in Washington. The big house is empty and Nancy and Stanley have lost contact with the nannies, sub-nannies, parlor maids, and butlers who once graced the airy, polished, flower-filled rooms. The use of the Gatehouse, however, belongs to them for life and they are free to wander over the well tended but deserted grounds.

It seems to me that the balance between artist and patron is in constant flux. On an invisible seesaw, money and the arts take turns: once Stanley and Nancy Young were up, now in many places it is wealth that plays host to culture. This occurred to me one night as I wandered around the immensity of the lobby of the New York State Theater during an intermission of the ballet. Gold is everywhere, as far and wide as the eye can reach. Tiers of golden mesh rise to the lofty ceiling and the small dark silhouettes of the crowd look like prisoners in a bejeweled Sing Sing pacing their golden-wired cells. Downstairs two gigantic white sculptured figures stand sentinel. Their immobile size, dominating the scene like a double version of the cemetery statue of the *Commendatore* in Mozart's *Don Giovanni*, presides over the gala exhibition — the explosive interplay between a plethora of wealth and a plethora of talent.

The public event that first brought to my attention a changed note in the age-old duet of artist and patron was the inauguration of John Kennedy. On television millions witnessed the new President taking office. It was a cold day in

Washington, and Kennedy, coatless, looked youthful and vital. As he spoke, his warm breath made puffs of vapor in the icy air. His guest of honor, the poet Robert Frost, appeared as old as Father Time himself. Shrunken inside his heavy wrappings he stood close to the small brazier that was unavailing against the sharp winter's day, and he recited his poem in a voice as feeble and intermittent as the faintly smoldering coals. The President's voice rang out with clarity and hope; he was the all-powerful host. Despite his obvious reverence for the age and genius of his guest, they reminded me as they stood side by side on the television screen of a crowned monarch and a wandering minstrel brought before him for his entertainment.

The salon of Winifred Root is another illustration of the workings of a wealthy culture professional. Through the door of her town house, renovated beyond recognition for her by a famous architect, pass the illustrious in all the arts. On her "evenings" she is to be found seated at the center of her brilliant circle, a massive woman as ponderously immobile as the sculpture that fills her rooms like a petrified forest. The stark white walls are hung with paintings by her protégés. Those unrepresented are scornfully referred to by her as "passé." Winifred receives in long medieval robes of costly brocade or velvet. She is past middle age and her cropped wiry hair is graying. She has the even features of a Roman emperor, and a bulging high forehead, and she continually mops her brow with an inadequate scrap of lace handkerchief as though she were helplessly overpowered by the electric vibrations of her inspired guests. Yet in her salon she is queen and the performance at her command.

A Russian poet has been reading his verse — rendered in

English, also, by a translator. The poet is dressed like a prosperous businessman in a black pin-striped suit. He has a
large head, swarthy and bald, and his eyes are as inscru-
table as a Buddha's. His translator, a professor of Slavic
languages from a midwestern university, is wearing a peasant
blouse in homespun fabric and sandals. The Russian de-
livers his poetry with passion — it is a call to arms, an invoca-
tion to a hidden Power. When he pauses, everyone is quiet
until the hostess breaks the spell. "It's just too much! I shall
be quite ill from emotion," she exclaims, mopping her expansive brow. She has, indeed, turned red and apoplectic as
though she had siphoned the fire of the artist into her own
veins, a difficult and painful procedure achieved at great
expense and at the risk of shattering her delicate sensibilities.
"Encore, encore!" she cries bravely.

The poet is reading his latest work, *My Country*, and I am
reminded of Stanley Young and of his and Nancy's court
in the Gatehouse — the Chinese calligraphy, the single
blossoming branch, the Bauhaus furniture, the smell of incense. Through the rolling cadences of the Russian poet I
am seeking the special intimacy of Stanley's voice, so long
ago, reading *America, My America*. I feel a moment's resentment of change. But perhaps nothing has changed very
much and I am regretting my own inability to strike gold
dust from the scene. And that magnetic tandem, Stanley
Young and Nancy Wilson Ross, was it in part my own creation, the result of an earlier, brighter vision?

CHAPTER VI

The Fan

THE SHOWCASES of our imagination are made one by one. In this way, a new creation coincides with the decline or extinction of an old one: I did not meet Charles Jackson until Stanley and Nancy Young had evolved into old friends. It would be incorrect to say that Charlie took their place, but he too, in his own way, represented for me that most real-unreal world of books and writing. Although he was at the height of his success at our meeting, I, changed by several years since my introduction to the Gatehouse at The Orchards, was no longer the hesitant acolyte before the high priest. With him I found the more intimate and different satisfaction of peer and confidant. He and I at first sight recognized in one another the perfect fan who had been lacking until then. Our enthusiasm was less for each other than directed together toward the masters we both loved. It was Mann, Proust, and Tolstoy who brought us close. From their fire, a flame enveloped us in mutual warmth.

These thoughts were with me as I sat in the church pew at Charles Jackson's funeral. For me, this constituted a double burial: the public service and my private, rueful observance of the death of a relationship that had begun to die several years before, slowly, almost imperceptibly at first but finally as irrevocably as the cessation of bodily life itself.

The church seemed inappropriate to the remains of Charles Jackson. Episcopalian, situated in a fashionable residential neighborhood of New York's East Seventies, it was homely, conventional, and frugal. Charlie would have wanted it to be gorgeous and historic. I would have wished for him an onion-domed cathedral, rich in gold and barbaric colors, with the snow falling outside and a mysterious woman, wrapped in dark furs and veiled, in a front pew — a St. Petersburg scene, straight from his beloved Tolstoy. Instead, the season was Indian summer and the church was hot and stuffy, upholstered in dusty red plush. The windows, by sealing off the daylight, allowed only a trickle of prismatic color to penetrate the box-like interior.

I looked around at the assorted gathering. In the first pew sat Charlie's wife and daughters, upright and correct as though at Sunday school, along with his remaining relatives from Newark, New York, his birthplace. Across the aisle was the young Hungarian factory worker with whom he had been living in a downtown hotel at the time of his death. His long, wavy blond hair, slicked down with water for the occasion, erupted here and there in unruly curls and his prominent cheekbones flamed, as though his shock and grief could not be tamed by the sanctimonious environment of the church. Scattered in the rest of the pews were fellow novelists, Hollywood script writers, editors, critics, and actors.

All were chapters in Charles Jackson's life: long or short, sad or comic, deep or trivial, linked together momentarily by the event of death. In which pew was the heart of Charles Jackson's existence located? It was impossible to say. Only his writer's imagination could have highlighted this one or that, with more drama than truthfulness. Who was Charles Jackson? Less than ever was I able to answer that question. As I passed in review the fifteen years of our relationship, it seemed that several human beings emerged under one name. As a farewell gesture, shutting out the droning minister and the people around me, I willed myself to remember, to assemble, as in an old-fashioned album, my collection of views of Charles Jackson. He would have enjoyed poring over them with me.

My first view had a summer's day in Marlboro, Vermont, for its setting. My husband and I were attending a writing and publishing seminar at Marlboro College. I remember the informal aspect of the place, white wooden barn-like buildings converted into a rustic academy, with scatterings of lecturers and students studding the lawn like dandelions. I had already been introduced to several important names who would be heading the seminar. There was the venerable if archaic German author, Ludwig Lewisohn, who had been a celebrity a generation earlier. He still retained a kind of embalmed renown, like the bust of a writer in a hall of fame. He was a slight, dignified figure, with an oversized head crowned by a shock of white hair like a maestro-conductor, and despite the heat and the bucolic surroundings, he was dressed in a formal dark city suit as though he were strolling down Berlin's Unter den Linden instead of squatting on the grass in Marlboro, Vermont. I remember Edmund Fuller, emerging professor and critic, and I also remember a middle-brow Catholic poet, acid-tongued, yet devout. She cultivated suburban domesticity and the literary life like the two sides of a penny, convinced that this common coin was one of rare mintage. My husband represented the publishing world. And the students composed the world of eager, would-be authors, confident that success could be acquired at writing seminars as women believe that beauty may be theirs by studying the models' faces in the glossy pages of fashion magazines.

I had been told that Charles Jackson was also present, the author of *The Lost Weekend,* a best-selling "case history" novel about an alcoholic. I had not yet met him but he had been pointed out to me, and when I went indoors on the morning of my arrival to telephone home to make sure that all was well with my young son, I was able to observe Charles Jackson through the window without his being aware of it. I cannot say why, but in that moment I sensed that this rather unimpressive-looking man was going to be important to me. The rural summer scene — the clusters of teachers and pupils, the shaggy grass, the old maples and elms — was the background and the window was the frame through which I was seeing him for the first time. He was small and plump in a neat buttercup-yellow Brooks Brothers shirt. He had an oval face with rounded cheeks, a shining, domed forehead, and a surprisingly long pointed nose like a sandpiper's beak. His mouth was shapely and sensual, a short black mustache set above it like a thatched roof. His almond-shaped eyes had a faintly exotic Tartar look as did his dark olive skin. But the overall impression was more prim than wild, and it was difficult to associate this man with the nightmare autobiographical happenings of his book. He had small, padded tan hands and he was wearing brown loafers, carefully polished to the color of a fumed oak sideboard. In spite of his meticulous grooming, he had the vulnerable, wistful air of a Charlie Chaplin tramp. (I could see him helplessly whirling around and around, trapped in some imaginary revolving door.) When I had reassured myself that nothing was wrong at home, I went out on the lawn to be introduced to him, with the distinct feeling that we knew each other already.

At this time he and his family were living in a spacious house in Orford, New Hampshire. It had the elegance and architectural grace of an eighteenth-century city dwelling but was located on a grass knoll in a country village. After the writers' conference at Marlboro our relationship grew rapidly and in spite of the many miles from New York City we were frequent visitors at Orford. After my husband became Charlie's publisher, we were members ex-officio of his family. He and his wife Rhoda always seemed totally unrelated. A native New Englander, she was as monosyllabic and repressed as he was voluble and dramatic. She was tall and straight, with wide features, a fair complexion, and smiling blue eyes that expressed endurance rather than merriment. The daughters, the oldest about ten at our meeting, and the younger, eight, divided their parents' traits. Sarah was tall and willowy, but she had her father's dark coloring and almond-shaped brown eyes. Kate was stocky and blonde, with her mother's glacier-blue eyes and pug features. But it was Kate who responded to music, painting, and books, while Sarah was literal-minded and practical. Oddly enough it was Sarah who was especially adored by her father. He delighted in telling anecdotes about her. "Sarah is a square," he would boast, and his eyes would melt as though he were in love. Often it is those most unlike ourselves who are the objects of our greatest passion, and Charlie never grew accustomed to the idea that he had sired this daughter. He would tell how when she was an infant in their grubby Greenwich Village apartment he would sit for long periods in perfect bliss with her tiny foot in the palm of his hand. "It was as perfect as a seashell, but warm, with a little animal life of its own," he would say. I knew that that baby's foot had been the most prized piece of his collection — and Charlie was a collector.

The house in Orford was full of paintings, antiques found at auctions, and expensively rebound volumes, his own included. He had designed a bookplate for himself ornamented with Shakespeare's head. Charlie fancied his resemblance to the Bard. He also collected autographed photographs of movie stars, including one of Judy Garland lovingly inscribed to him, and his reigning queen, Greta Garbo, whose image, increasingly beautiful, became more goddess than woman through the years. For me, the richest vein was his record library. To this day, when I hear the pellucid, gliding notes of Shubert's *The Trout*, I am brought back to those times with Charles Jackson.

The house itself was the most substantial object in the collection. He and Rhoda used to tell the story of how, when they were poor and struggling in New York City and Charlie was writing a soap opera serial, teaching night courses, and publishing an occasional story in the "little magazines," they would pass the elegant house perched on its knoll and he would vow, "When I'm rich, it will be mine!" After the explosive success of *The Lost Weekend*, it came true in fairy-story fashion. But, as in the fairy stories, the granted wish brought misfortune with it. The house in Orford was to be unlucky. Charlie took pride in displaying its fluted fan front door, its double curving staircase, its breezeway, the scenic wallpaper in the dining room. Its chief glory was the white colonial library, his study, where all his books were neatly arranged. His Early American desk was meticulously equipped with an assortment of pens, well-sharpened pencils, and the typewriter (as commemorative as a national monument) that had been used for *The Lost Weekend*. The window overlooked the single drowsy street of Orford with the Vermont hills beyond. But the tragedy of the library was that its owner was producing nothing there.

In the cramped, shabby city apartment, with success still a dream, he had written many stories about Newark, New York. He had taken an intimate backward look at the housewife gossips, the Sunday school teachers, the storekeepers, and the book-hungry adolescent who used to be Charles Jackson — who still existed inside the middle-aged man. In that uncomfortable flat he had dashed off the book that was to make him famous overnight, a savage, honest, despairing account of Charles Jackson, alcoholic. But here in Orford, in the house he had longed for, he could not write although his obsession with writing grew in ratio with his impotence. In these tranquil rooms the many Charles Jacksons co-existed, battling incessantly: there was the warm, proud father, the occasionally companionable husband, the unbridled alcoholic, the famous author, the clown, the irrepressible homosexual, and the generous fan. When we arrived for a visit we never knew which to expect. But these violent swings did not disturb me, nor did I feel pity for him. I was able from my vantage point, close by but on the sidelines, to observe him with interest and without condemnation — and, in his more congenial roles, to profit from him, knowing that he would never be still long enough to pall. We were able to talk for long, effortless hours, lighting up at the same topics, or to be silent together, letting the familiar phrases of *The Trout* or Beethoven's Archduke Trio, like an inspired, flowing conversation between friends, take up where we left off.

Sometimes upon arrival we knew that the visit would be turbulent. Charlie would greet us unshaven, wild-eyed, like a barometer, his appearance indicating stormy weather. No matter that our son or Charlie's daughters might be present; the family man had gone under. After the children went to bed, he would keep us up, talking tirelessly in his husky voice, the result of a bout of tuberculosis and a lung puncture when he was young. He was never loud, but curiously menacing and willfully self-destructive. The alcoholic and the homosexual at these times strutted exhibitionistically before the footlights, the husband, father, and friend having made an exit, seemingly never to reappear.

The next morning Rhoda, my husband, and I would come downstairs hollow-eyed and uneasy for breakfast with the children. But when Charlie made his appearance, he would look rested and rosy, ready to organize a family picnic. By the side of a brook, I observed him, plump and bald yet strangely youthful, dressed in a well-ironed pink Brooks Brothers shirt and the over-polished loafers. In the sunshine he was gaily helping the children to place bottles of soda pop and Coca-Cola in the cooling, shallow water, while the rest of us, dispirited, were laying out the hard-boiled eggs and picnic sandwiches on a blanket in the warm shade of the woods.

Our most dramatic visit took place shortly before Charlie, almost penniless again, sold the house in Orford. We had been witness to a long drunken evening and were at last in bed when we heard the loud strains of the *Liebestod* drifting up the stairwell, followed by a knock at our door and Charlie's soft, blurred voice: "I must talk to you. I am about to kill myself." My husband, up at once, called out, "I'll be right there!" But I did not move. For the first time, I had had enough. I did not believe in Charlie's suicide attempt. And the appropriate background music, in spite of its intrinsic beauty, perhaps because of it, sounded as tinny and tawdry as a juke box in a penny arcade. I lay, wakeful, listening to my husband's calm, reasoning voice. It was soon joined by Rhoda's pleading and over all floated the *Liebestod,* soaring in its unearthly beauty, sullied by the sham drama in the library below. Then there was a knock on the door again, and Charlie stood in my room, swaying and angry. "Why are you the only one not downstairs? Do you want me to kill myself? Is that it?"

Furious but unresisting, I got up and joined the others. We begged, scolded, reasoned. I still did not believe in the threat of suicide, but there was danger in the agitated, ugly person of Charles Jackson brandishing the bottle of sleeping pills as though it were a revolver. A shocking casualty seemed to have taken place already. It was light before he finally dropped the pills and we all mounted to bed.

In the morning we walked on tiptoe and whispered so as not to disturb Charlie. The children were admonished to be quiet: "Papa was sick during the night." When I passed his room, the door was ajar and, morbidly, I peeked inside. He was sleeping peacefully, a faint snore issuing from his sandpiper's beak nose and lifting his upper lip, with its Charlie Chaplin black mustache. He was lying on his back, clad in pink Dr. Denton pajamas, primly buttoned up the front, with feet, like those worn by children downstairs on Christmas morning to see the tree.

In spite of such deterrents our relationship went on, encouraged by the writing and receiving of letters. It seems to me, looking back, that our correspondence was as important as our meetings. His letters were long and crammed, festooned with postcripts and marginal additions in his round childish handwriting. They came thick and fast, and dealt with ideas for novels and stories, and his dreams. They were a link between the wonderful, unspoiled moment of the birth of an idea in an author's mind and the disappointing reality of the finished work. I do not know what literary rank Charles Jackson will hold in time or whether he will even be remembered. But of this I am certain: the stirrings of his imagination, whatever their results, were kindred to the masters he loved. And it was this aspect of his nature that created the joys and the miseries of his life. In his letters he would address me as Madame Straus, an allusion to Madame Straus, Parisian *salonnière*, daughter of Halévy and once the wife of Bizet, who had been for many years Proust's confidante and the recipient of much of his voluminous correspondence. It was a joke between us, but for Charlie it was the kind of play-acting he could not do without. The letters blur in memory and I wish I had saved them. I remember that many of them were about the great Russian writers; Bazarov, Natasha, Uncle Vanya, Prince

Andrey, Pierre, the Karamazovs, Anna, Vronsky were as real to him as his wife and daughters. The sleighs in the snowy streets of Moscow or St. Petersburg, the Rostovs' town house and the country retreat of old Prince Bolkonsky were more vivid than the hills of Orford, New Hampshire. I realize now that many of these letters were written late at night when he was drunk, that the wings with which he flew were often borrowed — for the courage he needed for his own work depended on alcohol — but no matter, he was writing. The letters to me often had a story or a book in embryo, offered like a pearl of rare price, and in this spirit I received them. They might read: "Madame, it is snowing outside, a whirling Moscow winter snow, and I have been sitting at my typewriter all night — nothing much produced yet, but an idea emerging that is for you alone . . . Do you like it? Whatever you say, I have the conviction that it will *be*, and telling it to you, dear Madame Straus, is a necessity. I have the title, already, *The Sunnier Side*. What do you think of it? I have written it twenty times over, the way I used to practice my signature when I was a school boy — and it looks great!"

Somehow, through the years, with the aid of alcohol, books were written again. But the tragedy of Charles Jackson was his first success; *The Lost Weekend* stood in the way of all that followed. Charlie was to remain a "lion" to himself and to take childish pleasure in imposing this image on his friends and family. "I took Sarah and Kate to see the display of the paper edition of *The Lost Weekend* at the Grand Central Station newstand," he related. " 'See, Papa is a famous man,' I told them."

I cannot count the times I sat beside him in the dark of

a theater while he quivered with pleasure at the film version of *The Lost Weekend,* as though the man in the audience had not created the happenings on the screen. There was Charles Jackson the awed fan, admiring Charles Jackson the celebrity and his inimitable success. But his response could also be intense when his own work was not involved. He never had enough of Greta Garbo in *Camille.* Every look from her famous eyes, every fold of her sweeping velvet gown, her voice, the love scenes, and her pitiful death were seen each time by Charlie as though it were the first. And his susceptibility was contagious.

I remember in particular a late spring day in New York City. We walked down Fifth Avenue, gala with flapping flags and new leaves appearing above the gray stone wall of Central Park. Charlie was dressed in a natty Glen Plaid suit, one of his pastel shirts, a precise bow tie like the pinioned wings of a butterfly, and a straw hat. He had developed a small potbelly, but it was not unbecoming; it looked rather cheerful, like his clothes and the sunny color of his skin. He was in an expansive mood. For him, that meant buying presents: a rare edition of Tolstoy's *Kreutzer Sonata,* lengthily inscribed, for me; a brass paperweight in the shape of a heart for my husband's office desk; a box of paints for Kate; a tiny enamel Russian Easter egg for Sarah, and a dress for Rhoda, who would accuse him, later, with some justice, of insane extravagance. But the day was glorious and nobody felt it more acutely than Charlie. We sat on the rim of the fountain in the Plaza among red and yellow tulips and young office girls eating their lunches in the sun. Sometimes we hailed a passing acquaintance who appeared as a minor participant in the festival we were sharing. Outside the Plaza

Hotel, the horse-and-buggies revived from their winter hibernation. The old drivers, wearing battered top hats like clowns, twirled their whips, and the garlanded carriages started off, bearing their passengers on a dreamlike tour of Central Park. Sitting on the edge of the fountain with Charlie I did not care that my holiday was unreal too, triggered by the weather and the scene, intensified by the alert antennae of the sad-comic little Charlie Chaplin man at my side.

The Jackson family moved from the large house in New Hampshire to a more modest one in Connecticut. Charlie frequently came to New York and our home was his base. His visits were electric and intimate, but they were often shadowed by the specter of drinking bouts. Yet even these times could have the sad-comic impress of his personality. He had been with us for a week and my husband and I watched helplessly as beer evolved into whisky and soda, then took a short cut to straight whisky. Charlie went from nervous, to expansive, to wildly witty, to maudlin, and then to virtual incoherence, his soft voice slurring words more and more until one afternoon he fell into a sodden sleep from which he was roused only to utter inarticulate sounds. We knew that he had an appointment for a lecture the next day and that it was vital that he should keep it, for funds were growing as short as the patience of Rhoda — who was trying to make ends meet in Connecticut while Charlie indulged himself in New York with theater, concerts, opera, shopping, and the endless talking to friends about his latest novel which he was neglecting to write.

We called our doctor to help us prop him up for his speaking engagement, but the doctor was old and autocratic, and answered, "I don't treat drunks." We tried several others until we found one who was willing to come. He arrived looking like an earnest student, in spite of his professional black bag. "I can't stand alcoholics," he echoed. "Where is he?" He consented to be led upstairs to where Charlie lay on the library couch. The doctor closed the door only to emerge an instant later fleeing across the hall to our bedroom like a startled deer. "I've given him something," he said, and from then on he directed the proceedings through us. We shuttled back and forth, delivering orders from him to Charlie, like middle men involved in a shady deal. At last, with our help, Charlie was able to stagger to his feet and the doctor promised to stay, in case of emergency, until we could get someone to escort Charlie to Vermont and his lecture engagement. Finally the four of us went into the dining room for an uneasy dinner, Charlie, the doctor, my husband, and I, mute with the awkwardness of our little party. It was Charlie, the patient, who carried off the occasion. Almost with admiration I watched him as he pretended to enjoy his oysters. I had divided the servings, originally planned for three, into four. The cool, slippery, pearl gray, spineless morsels in their shell cradles will always remind me of that evening. Charlie was unshaven, his shirt crumpled, but he was debonair and brilliant, giving us an account of his stay, many years before, in a Davos sanitorium for tuberculosis where he, an American rube, found himself in Europe for the first time, surrounded by the international glamour of his fellow patients. The anecdotes were both funny and pathetic, and it occurred to me that the middle-aged novelist had not traveled so very far from that boy from Newark, New York, staked to an expensive cure in Switzerland by a rich old man from the United States.

At last my husband tracked down an acquaintance willing

to be Charlie's traveling companion. When the door bell rang, we all, especially the young doctor, jumped up eagerly, like stranded explorers on a mountain top at the sound of the barking of the rescue dogs. Harl Cook was virile and handsome, still young, once a sailor, now a sometime writer, living on Cape Cod and picking up jobs around the boat yards. His blue eyes were set in creases put there by weather rather than age. He looked strong and confident, and like the doctor he was carrying a small bag.

"Let's get going," he said cheerfully, "or else this gentleman and I will miss the train."

Without more ado, he took his charge by the arm and headed for the door. Charlie looked up at him with obvious relief, and there was an expression in his almond-shaped Tartar eyes that reminded me of a young girl about to be whirled away by an attractive, sophisticated dancing partner, admiration mingling with an awakening attraction.

The next morning, Charlie appeared for his lecture none the worse for wear and Harl reported that the trip had been uneventful. "You know what I had in my little bag?" he asked. "A bottle of booze. Charlie and I had just one nip in the compartment before turning in — I'm an old hand at managing these types."

But sometimes the drinking bouts had more serious consequences. He had been with us and then had disappeared, and I knew his days and nights were like those he had re-created with so much success in *The Lost Weekend*. I telephoned Rhoda for advice and she directed me to pack his bag and put it next to the front door. "He'll come back, pick it up, and go again. You shouldn't have the responsibility for him at a time like this." Her voice sounded cool, experienced, and resigned. I packed Charlie's colorful shirts, his bow ties, and his pink pajamas in his valise. At the bottom of a bureau drawer I discovered a large bottle of seconal capsules, looking as innocent and cheerful as a jar of candies, but I realized their danger for him. He had graduated from alcohol to alcohol combined with barbiturates. I hesitated, but at last put the jar into the bag under the shirts and a cashmere sweater. It seemed an indignity to confiscate his belongings.

That afternoon when I returned home, the packed suitcase was no longer next to the front door. Charlie had come and gone. I breathed a sigh of relief. But upstairs, the door to the library — his room — was ominously shut. I knocked but there was no answer; I knocked again, more loudly — still silence. Inside, I found Charlie, apparently asleep on the couch. But this time he was not to be roused. I pushed and shook and called out, without effect. Then I noticed the bottle of pills lying on the floor, open, next to the sofa. A few capsules, like unstrung shocking-pink beads, had spilled over the carpet. I saw that the almost full jar was now almost empty. Frantic, I telephoned my husband, who called Bellevue Hospital. When the still unconscious Charlie had been loaded on the stretcher, a white sheet tucked up around his chin like a ruff, I was able to note in spite of my agitation that his disembodied head, bald and immobile, did indeed look very much like the engraving of Shakespeare on the bookplates in his library.

At Bellevue, Charles Jackson recovered once again. But this bout marked a milestone, because it was here that he met the young priest who caused his conversion to the Catholic Church. For months afterwards Charlie used to dramatize his awakening to religion. The day his instruction was completed, he put Sarah on a train for Connecticut with last-minute messages. "I'll be home for the week-end," he said, adding, "Be sure to tell Mama to have fish on Friday!"

Catholicism did not last long. It was followed by Alcoholics Anonymous, which proved more effective. Charlie traveled throughout the United States, lecturing. The outsider had become a team captain. Once I attended a meeting, startled to realize that the evangelist on the platform was the same man I had glimpsed twelve years earlier framed in a window at Marlboro College. His family and friends rejoiced at his new-found sobriety and I joined the chorus, although, looking back, I realize that this was the beginning of the diminution of our affinity. There were lapses in the cure, of course, but they were brief, and he would resume his lectures, more eager than ever to confess and to reaffirm his faith. But writing was put aside with alcohol. Charlie, for whom writing had always been a crazy leap, was grounded. The "perfect fan" dwindled also, and although when we met we still discussed Tolstoy, Mann, and Proust, it seemed as though we had said it all before. The man was gone who at his drunkest could identify himself with Moussorgsky at one moment, and yet at the next could sit on the edge of his chair at a performance of *Boris Godunov* like a child with all the world's pageantry spread before him. In his place I was forced to recognize a being I had not met before, the small-towner at home on the back porch gossiping about the neighbors.

My husband and I saw him less and less frequently. I was scarcely aware of it, so little did Charlie figure in my life at this time. But relationships of this order do not die a sudden death; they linger; like a chronic but hopelessly sick patient, they have their ups and downs on an always descending graph. One winter afternoon he called me. His voice on the telephone was more husky than ever, interrupted at intervals by choking paroxysms of coughing, the result of a recent lung operation he had barely survived — a drab but dangerous postcript to the "magic mountain" chapter of his life. Yet I could detect something of the old Charlie. "I've just sold a novel to a paper publishing house." (His first book in several years.) "I know it's a potboiler but guess what I'm going to do with the money? I have decided to take a trip to Russia!" I was aware that his family should have profited from the proceeds, but the vision of Charlie in the St. Petersburg and Moscow of his dreams — sick and solitary, but joyous and awed — revived my feeling for him. "You come, too," he was continuing. "Let's go together." He never got there. Perhaps it was just as well that the boundaries of his Russia should have remained inside the covers of a book.

Toward the end of his life, my husband and I were his guests at a downtown hotel where he was living with his friend. As in his house at Orford, Charlie showed us with pride around the premises. Here too he pointed out the staircase, not a chaste, white, graceful double arch but a grimy marble and wrought iron spiral, a leftover from the *art nouveau* era grown "camp" with age. From the top floor where Charlie lived, we peered down the deep, dangerous well that smelt faintly of stale urine. He pointed out the celebrities, his fellow lodgers at the Chelsea Hotel: a famous violinist and a famous painter, a choreographer, and an actor — but Charlie did not know them, he was a freshman admiring the seniors from a respectful distance.

In this apartment I recognized the remains of his more affluent days, like trophies in an archeological exhibition. I examined a large photograph of his roommate hanging on a wall in the bedroom. With his silver-blond hair, high cheekbones, and regular features, he might have been a youthful foreign movie star. But I knew that Charlie had picked him up in an all-night diner near the hotel, that he was simple and illiterate. To him, Charles Jackson was a dazzling celebrity and he the faithful servitor. Now, at the end of Charlie's career, this humble adulation was more vital to Charlie than home and family. Although he talked at length about this friend, we did not meet him. Perhaps he had left already for the Scotch tape factory where he worked the night shift.

The last time I saw Charlie it was from a sense of duty. It was August and he was alone in the hot city. His friend was on vacation. It was a sultry day and the Westchester countryside was dressed appropriately in limp, monotone, spinachy green. The air was a Turkish bath. Charlie arrived looking shockingly old and shriveled. One shoulder was lower than the other and his body listed at an acute angle, as though fixed in a lopsided bow to death. Like a child with a new toy he showed me the oxygen unit he had to have with him at all times. As a house present he gave me a Beatles record, his latest discovery. I thanked him, but this time I could not equal his enthusiasm, remembering nostalgically my discovery, so many years ago, of *The Trout* and the Archduke Trio. The evening was as lifeless as the weather. We exchanged snapshots of our granddaughters. It all had a hollow note.

The next morning was clear and cooler and Charlie appeared stronger. I waved him off from the top of the stairs as he and my husband stood below, ready to leave for the city. "Goodbye, Madame," he called cheerfully. Then, "I love you . . . Did you hear what I said?" he asked. "I heard you," I answered, and turned away without another word.

A few days later, Charlie's agent telephoned to tell me of his death from an overdose of sleeping pills. My husband was away on a business trip and there was no one else with whom I wanted to talk about Charles Jackson. I saw the house in Orford again, heard the record playing the *Liebestod* over and over — and saw the shocking-pink capsules spilled on our library carpet like scattered beads. Did Charlie, aging and ill, really wish to die? Or was it just another high wire act that this time he was too feeble to perform?

The funeral was over. I watched the family slowly following the casket up the aisle. What were they remembering? And his hotel companion? The tears coursing down his face were as plentiful and unselfconscious as rain.

After the dark of the church the day was blatant. As I walked toward home Charlie was with me, one shoulder raised with sick jauntiness — "Madame, I love you . . ." I had rebuffed him because I was selfishly intent on the preservation of my own image of Charles Jackson, more important to me than the human being whose insistence at that moment was an intrusion. The heat, radiating from the pavements and belching out of the exhausts of overworked air-conditioners, was a symbolic punishment. Yet I was comforted by the thought that Charlie, had he been aware of it, would have forgiven my transgression. Perhaps he, of all people, would have understood it.

CHAPTER VII

The Master of Finistère

FINISTÈRE was the most romantic house I ever knew. I speak of it in the past tense because it is empty now, bequeathed as a museum to the citizens of Port Washington, Long Island, as directed by the will of my husband's Uncle Rupert. True to its name, which means Land's End, Finistère was situated at the very edge of a cliff overlooking the Sound. Here and there could be seen triangles of sails and the choppy festoons of waves that murmured softly like discreet servants laying a carpet beneath the tall turreted walls of the house. It had been built by its owner around 1920. French Provincial, it was unrelated to the English castle on the same property where Rupert had spent his youth. That older dwelling, uninhabited since the death of his father, was made of gray stone imported piece by piece from England. Like imitation lords, its crenelated towers pompously surveyed the feudal acreage of the estate. Finistère, of Latin origin, was even less indigenous to Long Island, but it grew on top of its rock with authentic grace and authority.

The property was separated from the public road by a high grill enclosing woods, lawns, gardens, paddocks, and enough subsidiary lodgings to form a complete village. But these were scattered, partly concealed by old trees and winding paths. In the spring the ground was covered with daffodils, a golden sea leading to the cobbled front courtyard of Finistère. Here you were met by more flowers in great earthenware pots: lilies, fuchsia, and azaleas in the spring, geraniums and orange trees in summer, chrysanthemums in the fall. Lined up in double or triple rank, they resembled soldiers in brilliant uniforms. One wing of the house was the garage enclosing Rupert's shining cars, as the stables beyond sheltered his sleek thoroughbred horses. Opposite the garage was a swimming pool enclosed on four sides and set in the midst of blooming oleanders. The atmosphere in this court branching from the main court was hothouse — a Roman bath fit for the Caesars.

I see Rupert seated on the terrace at the back of the house high above the spread carpet of the Sound. Sea, sky, and sand seemed to repeat his own coloring as a symphony takes up a theme introduced by a few chosen instruments. Rupert kept his tan all year round, and his bald head and face were the color of tawny sand. His large eyes, the palest blue of distant waters, were set so deep in their sockets that they resembled aquamarines in dark cases. In the summer he wore a white suit contrasting with his sunburned skin, and a pastel blue shirt that imitated the extraordinary color of his eyes as the jewels painted by a master astound one by their similarity to the real thing. When he rose to greet us it was always a surprise to note that he was of somewhat small stature and delicately boned — so impressive was his figure against the sweep of sky and sea of Finistère.

At different times of the year various parts of Finistère presented themselves to my consciousness while others disappeared into shadowy recesses, captives in an oubliette. In cold weather we were kept indoors in the large drawing room paneled in oily dark wood, or in the den where through the closed windows and drawn portières I could hear the faint murmur of the waves like mendicants begging admittance inside the castle gates. Their sound made me nostalgic for summer when Finistère was in full glory. When it was warm, we met on the terrace to watch the sunset as if it were a private display of fireworks. Sometimes my husband and I would be alone with Rupert, at other times we would be part of a large gathering or family group. But whatever the number, Rupert maintained a gracious formality at Finistère.

He treated his three daughters with distant chivalry. Marion, the oldest, was fair, with her father's blue eyes, which looked surprisingly commonplace translated into her rosy round-cheeked face. Diana, the second, was dark as a gypsy. She and her sister were as prettily contrasted and multicolored as the porcelain fruits in the della Robbia garlands that adorned the halls of Finistère. But, as in the fairy stories, it was the youngest daughter, Penelope, who was the most beautiful, willow slim with long silky hair that fell across her delicate aristocratic face as she played the dulcimer in the drawing room or on the terrace for Rupert's entertainment. The offspring of his second marriage, she was almost young enough to be the daughter of her half-sisters.

During the last decade of his life Rupert was a widower. Before that I had known only Candace, his third wife, a coldly handsome woman with a cameo profile. He treated her like his daughters, with cool gallantry, but she, unable to accept the role of accessory as pliantly as they, grew to be a threat to the regime. Under the same roof she lived apart. Early in their marriage Rupert, fearing that she, much younger and childless, might grow bored, had bought a newspaper for her amusement. He had bestowed it upon her in the same spirit in which he had given her his mother's large black pearl, which Candace wore becomingly hanging from a velvet ribbon around her white throat. For her, however, the newspaper was no bauble, and like one of Rupert's pedigreed fillies she took the bit in her teeth, becoming a successful editor, the "boss lady" to the staff of her magazine and a total loss to her husband. But after two failed marriages each, neither Rupert nor Candace contemplated divorce.

I had observed that while Rupert addressed his family with reserve, his attitude to his servants was often warm and friendly. His voice was gentle when he talked to Tom, his tipsy old butler, Nora, the decrepit Irish waitress with crimped henna-dyed hair, Neil, his valet, or Malcolm, the chauffeur. But he held firmly the reins that controlled his entire staff, from the white-capped chef in the kitchen to the lowliest groom in the stable. I remember one summer evening when peace and order were reflected in the placid water, in the salmon-pink sky over which the last clouds were moving in stately procession, and in the sun, lowering its fading resplendence slowly into the horizon. Far below at the edge of the cliff we saw a fisherman in a rowboat. After pulling in his line he raised both arms in a triumphant salute to Rupert, who was leaning over the balustrade. "That man fishes here almost every evening at this hour," he said in his soft voice with a touch of unaccountable southern drawl. "We'll have his fresh catch for dinner," and he waved down to the gesticulating dot. Suddenly the steep drop looked less impregnable, as though the greetings exchanged — with pride below and appreciation at the top — were a drawbridge extended across the moat. Later we sat down to dinner in the summer dining room located in one of the turrets. Its circular stone walls were perforated by narrow apertures each presenting a view of sea and sky in perfect miniature. The newly caught fish was proudly carried in by Tom. It was laid out in magnificence on a silver platter and we ate it with the solemnity of celebrants of the Mass.

Sometimes I was shown the dark side of Finistère. After Hitler's defeat, Rupert, an aviator in the First World War, a commodore during the Second, had allowed the Navy to requisition his father's house for captive German scientists. One afternoon as we strolled in the direction of the old castle the clock in the central tower struck the hour. Chimes contain the past. For me they vibrated with half forgotten travels in foreign lands; for the distinguished hostages, each one a Dr. Faustus, they must have brought back their native German cities. But no robed figures of the Apostles made their appearance up in the clock tower; instead, a startled sea gull flew out from the ivy creepers and with a hoarse cry headed out for the sea, its gleaming wings outspread like an airplane. The castle was circled by barbed wire and posted with guards. The Gothic windows revealed no sign of life but I knew that behind the thick stone walls supernatural ideas were being hatched as in a Witch's Sabbath. This was a nursery of fledgling atomic monsters conceived and given birth to by the enemy for our usage in war. My husband was unusually quiet. Was he remembering the festive family gatherings here when he was a child in his grandfather's time? Only Rupert was undisturbed. The tycoon had been superseded by the warlord, the prisoners were his spoil, a conquest for the realm.

After Candace's untimely death, two changes occurred at Finistère: Rupert took over her position as editor of *The Record,* and his eldest grandson, Ian, recently come of age, made his appearance as heir apparent. By this time Rupert was over seventy, and it was surprising to see his enthusiasm for his new role as a working journalist. Although he now spoke reverently of his wife — homage to a dead queen — in taking over the newspaper with so much gusto he seemed to be burying all traces of her successful career. In his hands, *The Record's* point of view shifted from liberal Democrat to right wing Republican and any of Candace's staff who were not with him were soon replaced. Now on our visits to Finistère he and my husband discussed publishing, and it was hard to believe that Rupert's career had begun only with his old age. His intelligence and the obvious pleasure he derived from every detail of the newspaper's management made me wonder whether his grandfather, a railroad pioneer, and his father, the buccaneer-tycoon, had done Rupert a disservice in leaving him their fortunes.

Ian was often his grandfather's guest. Though quiet he was not ill at ease. He had Rupert's delicate aristocratic frame but his face was milder, partly hidden by a full brown beard and long straggling hair, from which his hazel eyes peered out as glossy as a squirrel's. One sunny July noon the four of us met for cocktails on the terrace. From where I was sitting the interior of the house looked cool and dusky, more mysterious than ever: a suit of armor partly glimpsed was a silvery shape in the living room, and I could see a curve of the mighty banister and a swag of curtain in a bedroom window high up under the steep slope of the black slate roof. On its pinnacle a rooster weathervane was silhouetted against the blazing sky. It did not seem to be indicating the direction of the wind but rather, like a sundial, to be casting shadows over the house to note the steady passage of time. Rupert was saying jocosely but with pride of ownership in his voice, "You didn't know that the Passion Play was in town, did you?" referring to Ian's beard and hair. In his T-shirt and jeans he did look remote from his grandfather's impeccable whites. But he was respectful and affectionate toward Rupert, calling him "Commodore" and listening to him with attention. Rupert continued, "This grandson of mine is going to learn the newspaper business from the bottom up so he can take over when I'm gone. I always say to him, 'Do as I say, not as I do.' He is also learning about horse breeding and about the management of the estate." Ian made no protest, he remained passive, but his bright squirrel eyes mutely registered a concealed life of their own. It must be far from Finistère, I thought.

Rupert's fantasy of succession ended. On his office desk at *The Record* he found a letter from Ian. It began "Dear Commodore," and its tone was mild, but it went on to say that he was resigning from the newspaper and that he renounced his interests in the breeding farm and the estate. He had decided, after much consideration, that this was not the life for him. He was going to be a painter. He regretted that he had not known his own mind sooner and he hoped that he was not causing Rupert pain . . .

Rupert related the content of the letter to my husband, his fury the more passionate for being quiet. "I offered him everything and that's the gratitude he shows me. I have already consulted my lawyers about changing my will. He will be cut off without a penny — let him starve in his filthy studio!"

He never saw his grandson again nor spoke to him although Ian made several gentle futile attempts at reconciliation. In his place Rupert acquired a brash young journalist and former White House aide, stepping down to make him chief editor of *The Record* with part ownership. He lavished on Frank all the frustrated hopes he had had for Ian. Frank became the son he never had, the appointed successor rather than the hereditary one.

Rupert was growing old. I noticed that his deep-set eyes were a more faded blue than his shirt and his tonsure more brilliantly white than his white suit. He often spoke about his will which he altered constantly, his plans for a foundation to study man's lust for power, and his decision to make Finistère a public park. He showed us the expensive photographs of the place in a catalogue: the house, its exterior, interior, courtyard, gardens, and view of the Sound. It was shocking, like a death mask portrait of someone who was still alive. Rupert was preparing for his demise in elaborate detail. With the cooperation of his sycophantic lawyers, he was building, codicil by codicil, his funeral monument — his Castel Sant'Angelo, the aging ruler's bid to immortality. His daughters hovered but he turned more and more to his trusty servants.

The last time I saw Rupert was not at Finistère but in Miami, where he went each spring for the races. This year he had sold his horses and was there as a spectator. It was Easter Sunday. The route to the motel where he was staying was blemished by grotesque concrete shapes: fake windmills, Hawaiian huts, Chinese pagodas, and a wild growth of condominiums as evil-looking as toadstools after rain. In my mind's eye I tried to replace them with the sea of daffodils and the winding shady road leading to the flowering courtyard of Finistère.

The lobby of the hotel resembled a funeral parlor. Bouquets of stiff gladioli and awkward furniture were grouped around a plastic mass of imitation driftwood. Neil, Rupert's valet, met us there. "The Commodore has been poorly lately," he said, "but he's feeling better today and is looking forward to your visit." Rupert's bungalow was on the beach but it was dark and furnished in the same expensive funeral-home fashion as the lobby. When we entered we found him sitting on an over-upholstered sofa under a framed reproduction of Van Gogh's *Sunflowers*. Although he was deeply tanned, his small head looked like a skull.

"Excuse me for not rising," he said, addressing me in his courtly manner, in that quiet voice with the touch of southern drawl. "My legs have been giving me a little trouble."

While he and my husband conversed I listened to the surf breaking on the beach, so much more overpowering and noisier than the whispering subservient waves of Finistère. When I returned my attention they were talking about *The Record*. Rupert looked unhealthily animated, his blue eyes in their hollow sockets had a febrile glow. He was saying ". . . so Frank thought he could take over the policy of the newspaper in anticipation of my death — filling it with half-baked Red propaganda. Well, I have shown him who is still master! I have just sold it from under his nose to a Republican middlewestern newspaper chain. Thank heavens I was spared long enough to make the deal. Such impertinence! Such ingratitude! I raised him up, now he can go back to where I found him. Before coming down here I consulted my lawyers about my will — "

Neil tiptoed into the room, "Malcolm is waiting out front with the car," he said servilely.

So Ian and Frank had both vanished. Marion, Diana, and Penelope had been kept at bay and here was Rupert, frail and weak like an old infant, attended by his valet and chauffeur. He grasped his cane and rose to his wobbling legs. It was then that I noticed the wheelchair, shining and well kept as the cars in Rupert's garage. With Neil pushing and my husband and me following, he was rolled through the mortuary planting of the patio garden of the motel.

Rupert was taking us for lunch to a German restaurant near the racetrack which he frequented. Always the host, he pointed out the sights in his seignorial manner. But the racetrack was a raw clearing in the condominiums and the restaurant smelled of sauerkraut and stale grease. Over our Easter Sunday lunch of wurst and mashed potatoes which none of us managed to eat, I wondered why Rupert, like Napoleon at St. Helena, did not die of his exile. I longed for the turret dining room with the narrow apertures displaying sea and sky like aquamarines and opals in a crown.

Uncle Rupert's funeral, although very different from Charles Jackson's, was equally inexpressive of the man himself. Before the rites, his family gathered in the musty antechamber of the Fifth Avenue synagogue. It was all strange to his Christian progeny. Marion, Diana, and Penelope, like white Russian émigrées in a shabby Parisian pension, received the chief rabbi and the Navy chaplin who were to officiate. Ian was conspicuous by his absence. The great main hall was packed with many of the city's prominent citizens. Rupert would have approved of that. But the pomp and ceremony were soon dispelled by the chatty tones of the rabbi and the chaplain, who vied with one another in colloquial informality. Although neither had met Rupert they spoke of him with intimate benevolence, praising his family relations and his charitable acts. They appeared inflated by their *ersatz* connection with him, but at each mention the chaplain mispronounced his name.

It was a raw gray February day, but as the hearse, the flower car, and the black limousines containing members of the family approached the cemetery, a pale silvery sun broke through the clouds. We wound our way through the overcrowded city of gravestones, elaborate and simple, old and new, all proclaiming the names of vanished Jews like a Diaspora of the deceased on the flats of Long Island. Could it be that Finistère was only a few miles off? How had Rupert traveled the road back so quickly? The cars stopped in front of the family plot; he was to be buried beside his mother. Inside the tent erected before the mausoleum, electric heaters were unavailing against the damp, and the steady drip of thawing snow accompanied the solemn intoning of the rabbi, grown traditional at the final step. The deafening explosion of a cannon shattered the hush, a last salute to the commodore from the Navy. A group of enlisted men came forward to fold back the American flag that had draped the coffin. Their gestures were as practiced and intricate as those of campers looping a Boy Scout's knot. Then the massive doors of the mausoleum opened, revealing a black shaft, and the master of Finistère joined his forebears.

After the funeral there was a great deal of scandalized discussion about the will. The foundation had triumphed. Marion, Diana, and Penelope were left a pinched portion of their inheritance. Some relatives claimed that Rupert had been senile when he signed the final codicil, others said that his enlarged vanity had created the bloated amorphous foundation to outlast him like the Sphinx. But I believe that Rupert, a King Lear in reverse, disinherited his dutiful daughters in order to pull his world down with him — to put an end to the doomed feudal lifestyle that had been his.

For me nothing remained of Finistère but the four pots of oleanders Rupert gave us many years ago. Transplanted to the corners of our pre-fabricated pool, they look more exposed and meager than their kin that flourished in the luxurious enclosure of a Roman bath. Yet I sometimes wonder how our son views our own way of life and how it will be remembered by our granddaughters. It is possible that at some future time this house too will represent the passing of an old order — that it will spell out a story almost as colorful and romantic as the one Finistère told to me.

CHAPTER VIII

The Studio

FOR A WHILE oleanders meant Finistère, then gradually it faded, no longer recalled by the slender trees growing top heavy in their wooden buckets. The dry spiky olive-green leaves, shimmering heat made solid, the bouquets of pink and white blossoms like little girls in frilly summer dresses rejoicing at another summer, came to signify, for me too, merely the return of the torrid season.

But since I have seen Rome the oleanders have become its ambassadors. Sometimes a fallen leaf spear or a frail flower will merge with Rome's profusion. I remember a trellised outdoor café where the oleanders bloomed. Here, above the Spanish Steps, the panorama of the city has been spread forever. A wealth of tropical vegetation grows between the crevices of ochre and rosy stony walls and in the distance across the wide sky clouds are swarming around the monumental hive of St. Peter's dome. From a single oleander leaf or blossom my memories of Rome unfurl.

My introduction to the city was preceded by my first transatlantic flight. Gone were the plodding ocean voyages with their heady detection of land, a fuzzy ridge on the horizon after seven days of watery monotony. Instead the trip has dwindled to a brief confinement in a capsule, a whiff of anesthesia between take-off and descent, and two identical airports appointed in the same hospital chrome, plastic, and miles of rubber flooring, with the same bland loudspeaker voice announcing arrivals and departures in several languages, all of them slightly off key. Destination, once a treasured goal, has been dissolved like a particle in a test tube. Only the excitement of motion remains.

I arrived numb, half awake. The sticker, *Roma,* on our suitcases reassured me that I was indeed there. The taxi ride from the airport was no different from the throughway at home. As the lights clustered more densely I realized that we were nearing the city. At a traffic stop the taxi halted and I got out to stretch my stiff legs. Great stone columns pockmarked by age rose into the night sky. Nearby the white phosphorescent plumes of a fountain were splashing into a basin. The present lost its opacity and I became one with a line of pilgrims stretching back into the infinite past, standing on this very spot, in awe like me, before the sight of enduring stone and the sound of water's perpetual play.

When we started off again the taxi driver said "Pantheon," in the same offhand voice as when a moment later, driving under a porte-cochère, he announced, "Hotel Excelsior."

The next morning my husband and I sat in the lobby to wait for Carlo Levi. The revolving door spun again and again, admitting robed cardinals like a flock of scarlet flamingos, an Italian film star and her retinue, an American family — mother, father, brother, sister — followed by mounds of luggage reminding me of my former travels, some business men, nuns, a photographer weighted with equipment like a scuba diver. Around and around again — more luggage, some German tourists, a prelate in purple — once more — and Carlo Levi was at last advancing toward us. He was dressed in a flowing black Svengali cape; his gray hair, long and curling, was as thick as a mane, his body as wide and solid as a tree stump. He had a massive head, aquiline features, and prominent, benign gray eyes, and his smile of greeting revealed jagged teeth. Rugged and shaggy, calm and confident in his earthy strength, Carlo Levi emerged from the city streets outside the revolving door like the wolf of Rome himself out of antiquity, into the lobby of the hotel.

As we squeezed into his diminutive car, his solid presence seemed to fill it to overflowing and I wondered how I would manage to see Rome through its small windows and across his wide shoulders. But limitations frequently prove to be assets, just as a brief, strictly metered poem may condense a universe and as, for me, some columns and a single fountain offered up to the moon had stood for all of Rome, so now my intercepted glimpses of the city exhilarated me and gave me a sensation of instant intimacy and challenge, like love at first sight.

It was Christmas day and raining but through the gray dampness the reds and yellows of old stones bled and glowed like living flesh and blood made lasting. We passed the Aurelian Wall, a survival from antiquity. It was still inhabited: someone had placed a pot of geraniums in a saucer on a window ledge, a brave orange banner against implacable age. In a medieval section of the city the narrow streets were filled with holiday makers, and Carlo Levi's car seemed to swell, barely allowing us passage. The high buildings on either side exuded a smell blended of food, crowded humanity, and something rotted, as though living and dying had intermingled and the simple people living here had learned to accept the blend as their daily fare. To honor Christmas, in front of the butcher shops, the *bécasses*, tiny bird carcasses, hung limply from their twig-like legs, their glassy eyes a mild reproach to feasting. Levi drove imperturbably, managing to avoid the darting cars from all directions. He let us out at the Piazza Navona, like a vast oblong drawing room walled by the façades of baroque churches and *palazzi* and furnished with Bernini's exuberant fountains — marble sea gods and monsters voluptuously entangled in bowers of spouting water. The sights multiplied: classical ruins yielding to the early Christian Middle Ages, to the Renaissance, to the modern world. Carlo Levi shepherded us through the city — extensive in depth, in time, rather than in breadth, in space. Rome is a deep ditch in which layers of civilization are preserved and utilized. Like the life-in-death figures on an Etruscan tomb, it has enshrined mortality and made it lovely. But a calm voice and knowing eye were necessary against the welter of impressions, making the descent into time's hole less precarious.

We lunched at a cave restaurant below street level, the spot where Caesar was stabbed on his way to the Senate. Levi tucked the generous napkin under his chin in preparation for his attack on the *bécasse* on the plate. Its glassy eyes had been removed in the kitchen. Although Carlo ate with gusto, I shrank from the feeling that we were all witnessing a pagan sacrificial rite. After lunch, as we were lingering over our espresso, the owner of the restaurant appeared shyly to greet Levi. He was still wearing his blood-spattered cook's apron and was followed by his black-eyed wife and numerous black-eyed progeny. *"Buono Natale, maestro,"* he said, pushing forward his oldest daughter. "She wants to show you her painting." Reluctantly the young woman placed her attempt before him. Carlo Levi, successful artist, author of *Christ Stopped at Eboli,* read in every country, was called upon to judge. But as he chewed upon the moist black stub of a cigar his kindly probing gray eyes reminded me of a country doctor or a parish priest, familiar, rotund, well-fed, and re-assuring, paying a leisurely visit to a poor family who assembled around him with all the warmth of proferred Christmas wine.

When I attempt to recall that first day in Rome I see a jumble of mosaic-like color, but a single patch of drabness persists: damp crumbling walls, pale gaunt faces, somber hollow eyes — Rome's ghetto — a constricted maze of alleys surviving intact from the Middle Ages. Levi piloted us through this nether region. It was almost deserted. Occasionally an emaciated figure would emerge with a ghost face and grieving eyes that seemed to be hoarding in their depths the whole tragic story of Jewish exile. Levi conversed with a boy wearing the traditional yarmulke. He was as at ease with him as he had been earlier with the restaurant keeper and his family, and gradually the youth began to thaw as though a stray chink of sunlight had penetrated this dungeon city within a city. Carlo Levi, the benign country doctor or parish priest, was now an Old Testament prophet empowered to transform humility into pride and endow a Roman ghetto with the dignity of a historic Jewish homeland.

After that Levi always received us in his studio. Year

after year my husband and I climbed the hill in back of the Piazza del Popolo to Via di Villa Ruffo, numero 31. Here in the heart of the hot city we found a wood as hushed and refreshing as a shaded pool. I seem to remember a perpetual summer, though the seasons were marked by small changes like vivid threads woven in the deep green of a forest tapestry: heavy hanging wisteria draping the studio windows like succulent grapes, a dappling of old gold in the fall, and the white touches of birches like a scattering of unicorns. After ringing the bell of number 31 we generally waited. Carlo Levi never hurried, time did not count, for him there was only the calm beneficent moment to profit from. We would hear his ponderous step and then we would be admitted inside the studio, always cool as a cellar. And Levi's smile, revealing his jagged wolf's teeth, was like a second door opening on our return.

My memories of that studio have been reinforced by so many lengthy visits that its properties have become mine, the furniture of my own mind. At the entrance, the first impression after the cellar-like coolness was of obscurity, clutter, and — overall — that haunting smell, an amalgam of wood shavings, turpentine, and paint common to painters' studios, so that I would become confused, believing myself to be back in another atelier in New York City. The other one has been dismantled, its owner is dead, but at number 31 Via di Villa Ruffo, it revives in me causing me, like someone waking in a new room, to ask myself: what's wrong? That tall window belongs here, not there, the easel should face this way, not that, and the stairs to the open-balconied bedroom floor are mounting in the wrong direction. Then gradually, like someone growing fully awake, I realize where I am.

Both my husband and I are warmly, ceremoniously embraced on both cheeks by our host, who leads us in single file through the welter of canvases, stacked, crated, rolled, spread out, and hanging. But the congestion is not confusing, it has the profusion and richness of nature. There is a sameness to the paintings: the landscapes fanciful and swirling, the portraits (they are the majority of Levi's work) somber and strong, all the faces stamped with peasant sternness, like excrescences of dour rocky land. These vital tragic heads are the imprints left on their creator's imagination by his year in Eboli as a political prisoner of the Mussolini regime. It was a rewarding accident that Levi was able to plunder, making use of it for all his days. Because he had been a doctor in his youth in Turin, he ministered to the poor people of Eboli, his flock, giving and receiving strength in their bleak God-forsaken country. In return they supplied him with a rich vein for his paintings and for his famous memoir, *Christ Stopped at Eboli,* a classic in its own time.

He led us to a small light clearing beneath the studio window looking out on the quiet wood. He would sit on the sofa like an indulgent father — or *il papa,* himself — and we would flank him on either side. He would be wearing a bright flower-sprigged shirt and a velvet smoking jacket over which his curly gray mane fell incongruously, like the wolf of Rome in fancy dress. His benevolence was steady as well as the ripe wisdom in his eyes. He would often talk about Eboli, pointing out with the pride of a man too comfortable inside his own skin to bother with modesty that his book was already a mythology — "I am the Homer of Calabria." At other times he would discourse on world events. To his numerous other professions he had added that of Communist senator. But he assimilated this latest career without fuss or hurry, with the same placid pleasure with which he ploughed through a heavy five-course meal. His activities increased like his girth, and his poise, like his digestion, was not disturbed. He told us about his travels, his semi-official visits to Russia and China. It seemed to me that the Communist leaders under his calm gaze must grow tame like lions changed into friendly dogs. "In China I saw the most marvelous display of fireworks," he said. "Voom, voom, voom! What a spectacle!" Levi's keen intelligence was tempered by a child's sense of wonder.

On one of our visits to Rome we found him preparing to leave for Palermo to assist at a hunger strike there. "Please come with me," he begged. "It will be very interesting." But we preferred to remain in Rome, our time being short; also I had come to resent the long hours at the studio which made it even shorter. Much as I had grown to love Carlo, he who had been my first guide had become my warm-hearted jailer, and the studio, a familiar prison, barred me from the life exploding outside. I might be walking in the sunshine on the Palatine Hill discovering small flowers pushing their way out between ancient stones; I could be absorbing that farflung view of the city from the Janiculum while I listened to the weirdly rural clucking of a hen in a farmyard nearby; or, rounding a corner, I might come upon the lush surprise of an inner court vivid with mosaic, palm trees, and marble fountain, like a fabulous mirage invented by a weary traveler. All this might be mine while I sat captive in the cellar-damp studio hour after hour listening to the endless stories of my jailer, who was as unaware of my restlessness as he was of the relentless forward motion of the hands of the clock.

As with many of his fellow Romans, the morning did not exist for Carlo. No one could reach him then, but during the leisurely lunch, which was generally served around three in the afternoon, the telephone would ring constantly. He plodded back and forth from the dining room to his adjacent bedroom and his familiar *"Pronto"* was an accompaniment to our repasts, as habitual as the strains of the violin playing Viennese waltzes in the dining room of the Hotel Excelsior.

At night he was indefatigable. I have an indelible vision of him in the salons of his wealthy friends. A bachelor, he was in great demand. I see him like some sybaritic god, shaggy and rough, gentled by the attentions of a hostess plying him with rare wines and viands, surrounded by women's graces drawn to his power and sweetness. I see the scene like a cornucopia overflowing with glowing fruit, and the strong, satiated wolf-god at its center; Carlo Levi was a Rasputin, replacing evil with good and sickly metaphysical trances with the secrets of wise living on this earth.

On his return from Palermo, he asked me to sit for a portrait. Through the years the accumulated faces of his many friends, the visiting great and the inhabitants of Calabria had combined to form a pictorial journal in the studio. I was to join the rest. He assured me that one afternoon would be sufficient. He placed me on a high-backed chair and I watched him behind his easel. He had removed his velvet smoking jacket for a coarse blue smock. His keen gray eyes kept traveling from his canvas to my face, as warm and no more penetrating than when there was no easel separating us, and his monologue was no less fluent. He told me about the strike at Palermo. "Everyone gathered in the square. The good poor people lay on straw pallets all night under the stars. There were speeches — I said something too — poems were recited — there was singing and the cheering of the strikers. What a rousing sight! I wish you had been there with me." His calm voice was conjuring up a scene from grand opera, not my picture of a hunger strike.

Now and then he would be called away to the telephone and I would hear the inevitable *"Pronto"* and that Italian small talk that sounded like poetry to my ears. The interruptions disturbed neither his discourse nor his painting. As the afternoon wore on I began to feel that I had been enthroned, listening forever while beyond the blinding studio window Rome throbbed, calling me outside to attempt to solve the riddle of its lure like many wayfarers before me.

Carlo would not be hurried. His patient maid of all work approached him again and again, holding out his coat and hat. "You'll be late for the meeting at the State House, *Senatore.*"

"Don't worry, Lucia, I will soon be finished," he said, smiling mildly and making no move to take off his smock. At last he put down his brush and palette. *"Finito.* Do you wish to see yourself?"

I walked around the easel and confronted my portrait. The face was shaded by my large leghorn straw hat outlined against an abstract background delicately tinted, suggesting a summer garden. But beneath the wavy brim my eyes looked out, startlingly unfamiliar, with the stern tragic expression of the peasant women of Eboli.

"I'll call a taxi now, *maestro,*" Lucia said as she helped him lovingly into his coat.

"Not just yet. I must first fetch — " and Carlo disappeared up the ladder stairs, agile despite his weight, into the bedroom.

He returned carrying a statue, almost life size, carved out

of sugar. In crude colors it represented a knight in armor. "This is for you," he said. "I brought it from Palermo. Sugar is their industry and they make these for Saint Days. I had a little difficulty with it on the plane: although I kept it on my lap his head broke off. See, I have mended it. It's as good as new."

Overwhelmed, I was at a loss for words. I was leaving for the United States the next day; how could I travel with this giant offering? "Thank you, Carlo, for your thought of me," I said, "but it will be impossible to take it with me."

We kissed au revoir on each cheek and I left him still holding the sugar knight.

Back home, I reviewed the episode with regret, wishing I could play the scene again and change the ending. I would take the knight away with me. For some reason, the colorful sugar sculpture, offered in warm impetuosity, has come to mean Italy. Why had I, the stiff unresponsive alien, refused it? And Rome — it is no longer returned to me with the sight of oleanders, the sound of church bells, but with that familiar smell, an amalgam of wood shavings, turpentine, and paint.

CHAPTER IX

The Real Unreality

Like Rome, opera came to me recently. My love affair with it should have started years ago but I was middle-aged and inexperienced when I succumbed with all the awkward ardor of the late initiate.

Wagner was my introduction and perhaps a cause for my retardation. It seems to me that one should not begin with him. He should enter at a later stage like an overwhelming Teutonic invasion after Latin culture has had its day. But when I was a child in the early thirties in New York City, Wagner held sway at the Metropolitan Opera House and Kirsten Flagstad was the reigning queen. My mother, a quasi-professional singer herself, an inconspicuous member of a choral society, felt that seeing Flagstad as Isolde was necessary to my education. I was drawn to the legend of *Tristan und Isolde*. I could picture the bleak corner of rocky Nordic coast warmed by passionate love and tragic death, via a magic potion. I saw Isolde, a slender reed shaken by the tearing gales of her kingdom, by marriage and by the onslaught of first passion. The elegance of the old Metropolitan Opera House was a richly contrasted setting for the jewel it was about to offer me like an uncut diamond, alternately dark and sparkling, displayed against the smooth red velvet cushions of a jeweler's box. I shivered in anticipation as I waited for the great golden curtain to part. The prelude added to my mounting fever. At last the opening scene was revealed; the billowing sails and deck of the galley bearing Isolde from her home in Ireland to the realm of King Mark, her betrothed, was all I had imagined. But where was Isolde?

The act was well advanced before I realized that the stout lady with the woolly flaxen braid who was standing so solidly planted on the sloping deck was indeed the legendary Irish princess. And the barrel-shaped gentleman with bandy spindle legs who swaggered and gesticulated as he sang represented the young lover, Tristan. At the close of the act, after the love potion had been quaffed and Tristan and Isolde had staggered into each other's arms, I failed to sense the birth of love — rather, I experienced the death of my expectations. I was like a passenger who cranes and strains to see out of the window of an airplane after the pilot has announced, "Ladies and gentlemen, we are now flying over the spectacular Alps. On your left you will note majestic Mont Blanc," — only to discover a few white-capped wrinkles in the land far below resembling a relief map in the schoolroom. So now, though scale had been increased rather than reduced, I suffered a similar disappointment. Without disputing the glories of the soprano, I did not feel what had been predicted. I laid the blame on myself, and like someone with faulty vision or hearing, I was apologetic, pretending to see what I did not see, hear what I did not hear, to be in the know — while my awakening to opera was postponed for many years. When it did happen, it would come as a surprise comparable to the astounding accident of love.

Occasionally I returned to the Metropolitan for more Wagner. The red velvet full dress of the opera house never failed to please me. From my place, usually in the orchestra, the box holders sparkled like the intricate jeweled works of my father's pocket watch when he opened the golden lid for my delighted inspection. But I no longer hoped to be moved by the happenings on stage. Without flinching I beheld Elsa on her wedding night in *Lohengrin*, another stout lady in a complicated artificial yellow wig (borrowed it seemed from Isolde), wearing a white satin nightgown glinting like snow across her mountainous bosom as she sang the beautiful faintly familiar love music with gestures worthy of Brutus addressing the Roman Senate. And Lohengrin — that unearthly bridegroom — was played by the barrel-shaped tenor I had seen as Tristan. When the swan appeared like an overblown bath toy, I felt it must collapse beneath his weight until I discovered that the singer was only walking beside it, his bandy legs concealed by the bird's sheltering white wings as he kept step with its jerky mechanical progress across the rear of the stage.

One summer in Salzburg, when I was eighteen, the reality of opera almost broke through my prejudices. It was the Toscanini era. In restrospect, I wish I could turn back the clock and experience all of it again, substituting my present ardor for past indifference. When I hear others talking about those days in Salzburg on the eve of World War II, I feel as though, only half-awake, I had participated in the Golden Age. True, I did appreciate the location: the almost operatic setting of the Austrian town with its small onion-domed churches, dark forests, greenish river, and the gray drizzling days that were not dull but like a darkened theater at the moment before the curtain rises. In the glimpsed figure of the Maestro there was electricity also. From a distance I admired his trimness, his deep black eyes, and the verve of his twirled white mustache. The Fest-Spiel-Haus looked simple, almost rustic after the Metropolitan, but the atmosphere was exalted like a congregation converted in music. It was during the last act of *Die Meistersinger* that my resistance to opera threatened to weaken. I had watched the endless preceding acts with my accustomed apathy. But all at once when Charles Kullman, as Walther, stepped up on the platform erected on stage for the song contest, the Nürnburg townfolk and the richly robed medieval guild members blended into a whole. Walther's resplendent array, the pure triumphant opening notes of the Prize Song, gold and white, transported me beyond the theater, beyond my paltry resistance into a new morning of sound, sight, and feeling. But it was quickly over. I was like a confirmed ascetic who has just enjoyed a *cordon bleu* meal in spite of himself, but is convinced that his pleasure was derived from other sources, the company or the sunset outside the restaurant's window. So now I preferred to tell myself that my excitement was simply a contagious symptom caught from the aroused audience surrounding me, rather than the direct response to the powerful ray of opera itself.

As time passed, I attended opera less and less frequently. I lost my apologetic attitude and I can hear myself saying, quite idiotically, with the voice of someone I do not know, and certainly would not wish to know, "Opera is not for me. It's like chicken in parts — neither music nor theater."

Later after I had fallen in love with Rome, I took Italian lessons in a vain attempt to keep the city close to me. I would approach the American Academy of Languages with a lift of heart thinking about glowing, ruddy stone walls, small burdened donkeys moving beneath contorted umbrella pines, and water falling over exuberant marble forms. The Academy always erased these visions. It was an inconspicuous building on East Fifty-seventh Street, airless and smelling of blackboard chalk. As soon as I entered I wondered why I was there and I had the instinct to flee. With my teacher, a depressed young lady from Tuscany (I had the feeling that our lessons heightened her morbidity), I would go over the tongue-twisting declinations I had studied during the week. My memory occupied with these schoolgirl tasks had no room for Rome, and the more I absorbed the grammar book, the farther I seemed to be from the possibility of conversing in Italian, even for the small speaking part assigned to me at Via di Villa Ruffo 31. One day my instructress announced that I was ready to attempt to read out loud from an Italian novel. I began — and as in a bad dream, helplessly, I heard my own voice distorting the language. Looking up from the page, I caught the expression on my teacher's face, I thought I even detected a moistness in her eyes, like the involuntary tears produced by the pain of the dentist's drill. I returned no more to the American Academy of Languages. Rome would have to be recaptured by some other means.

When a friend invited us to see Verdi's *La Traviata,* starring Maria Callas, I accepted, pleased that I would be hearing good Italian again. Also I could put my lessons to some use. Like someone lost in a foreign city who is able to read a few signposts, I might be able to translate the *addios, ascoltos, evvivas* of Italian opera. The night of the performance found me unsuspecting.

I had heard the prelude but I was seeing a Verdi opera for the first time. The curtain rose on the party scene. As Violetta circulated among her guests, her feverish gaiety entered into me. I followed as if she were a mote of light dancing inside the suffocatingly ornate setting, beautiful and damaged, triumphant and doomed, acutely alive yet with death hovering near, at once the embodiment of idealistic love and a nineteenth-century Parisian demimondaine. The action might be trite, the story shopworn, but through the medium of Violetta-Callas, at one with the music, my immunity was disintegrating and opera was penetrating my very core. She and the music cast a spell that seemed to be saying: I reveal the human soul stripped of its outer wrappings, free from the pettiness of living. I am the expression of life itself. Gaiety, Jealousy, Sorrow, Desire, Fear, Joy, Hope, Love, Hatred are all archetypal shadows, more lasting than the shallow vessels containing them. As long as the music endures you will be empowered to recognize them — real unrealities — but when the spell is broken, you will be returned to the small preoccupations of individual existence ...

As often as possible I saw Callas in her various parts and always the physical presence of the diva — the great sweeping eyes like bat wings, the strong mobile features, the Nefertiti head and pliant body — lost its identity in the role she was playing. Yet after that night at *La Traviata* I was able to watch the more opaque performances of other singers with almost equal joy. The showcase of opera was open: Verdi and Callas had presented me with the key.

Autumn is the season of promise in New York City. I

have always felt it, I still do. One afternoon driving west across town to Lincoln Center, I sensed a lift in mood that had no connection with my destination, which was a master class given by Maria Callas at the Juilliard School of Music. She had retired from the opera stage and, while her fellow singers were performing nearby, she was now limited to the role of teacher. Loyal to the awakening she had caused, I felt that both she and I were being cheated. But my friend, the poet Ned O'Gorman, had managed with difficulty to obtain two places in her class, which was not meant to be a demonstration for the public. Opera, however, was not in my thoughts as I drove; I was struck by the late afternoon light gilding the skyscrapers surrounding Central Park. Pedestrians, bicyclists, the old and the young appeared to be moving in unison to an accelerated rhythm. Heavy-footed summer had been routed once again — it was October, the zestful, the productive, the irrationally hopeful month in New York.

I was early so I waited among young Juilliard students lounging around the entrance to the auditorium. They were beautiful with their long hair and folk festival dress, as graceful as shepherds in a painting by Raphael. Ned O'Gorman was running toward me; he too seemed to be responding to the shared rhythm. I saw him in sharp clarity at that moment. Although this chapter belongs to Maria Callas and to opera, his image intrudes, it insists on being present. And since random memory is my guide, I follow its lead, collecting the haphazard gifts that it drops in its wake, confident that they are all connected by a filament too delicate for my reasonable mind to detect.

Ned is tall and strong; about forty, he looks surprisingly boyish as he bounds along the pavement like someone country bred. His cheeks glow as if he had been pitching hay in an open field. Instead, he is arriving directly from his Storefront in Harlem. It is a school for young children started by him, where he gives his gargantuan energies and his big heart to his infant charges, tiny injured sparrows caught in the city's cruel maw. He heals with an imagination that is still close to childhood. He has tried the theater, attempted the priesthood, but he found his place with children, writing poetry in his spare time. His books are enriched by his life in Harlem as the children gain from his poet's responsiveness. As he approaches, his deep-set clear blue eyes under jutting black brows seem to light his path like a flare. They say more than most eyes: they belong to the flawed saint, the hedonist, gentle healer, angry fighter, the sage, and to someone clamorously aware of beauty whenever and wherever he may uncover it.

Ned is an opera lover but he has never seen Maria Callas. In our places inside the auditorium I try to tell him what she has meant to me. The stage contains only a piano, a microphone, and a high stool. I wish for the elaborate sets of *La Traviata* or the church and crenelated parapet of the Castel Sant'Angelo in *Tosca*. The accompanist arrives and seats himself at the piano, waiting. Someone else has appeared. She is straight and thin and is wearing flowing hostess pajamas; her long brown hair falls abundantly over her shoulders, pulled back from a severe, almost plain face. When she puts on owlish spectacles, she is a stylish school teacher peering into the front rows of the orchestra where the students are seated. "Who will begin today, *hein?*" The voice is vibrant with an indefinable foreign accent. It is Maria Callas speaking.

A fat blonde girl steps up to the stage. She is dressed in

a mini-skirt that reveals her pudgy thighs and knees like baked potatoes. She confers with Callas and the accompanist strikes the chord for the opening of an aria from *Norma*. The blonde girl sings with a large voice. Callas is perched on the stool, every angle of her body listening. Occasionally she interrupts the aria. ". . . but you must make it more *legaaato* . . ." With a nod to the pianist, she indicates that she will sing the aria herself. Standing on the nude stage, she makes no gestures but the magical voice once again conjures up the overpowering archetypal shadows. The school teacher had vanished and in her place is Norma, the beautiful Druid vestal virgin, proud and passionate. When the aria ends, I glance at Ned. His eyes are phosphorescent in the semi-darkness, his arm on the rest between us, tense. The blonde girl with the baked potato knees tries again and Callas returns to her listening perch on the high stool.

Another student steps up; she sings Mimi from *La Bohème*. When Callas takes over this time, her sophisticated costume seems to change into the romantic rags of the Parisian soubrette, the severe profile grows young and tentative. *Aida* follows, even the male role of *I Pagliacci*. Callas is not impatient. Just once, halting a flamboyant redhead performing the mad scene from *Lucia di Lammermoor*, she inquires, "You're not feeling well today, *hein?*" The student is suitably felled but bravely tries again. Callas is painstaking, encouraging, soberly absorbed in the music. She bends over a page, "Always follow the composer," she says. "The score is the master." She is no diva now, brilliant and imperious. I see a new Callas, not transfigured by a role but by her dedication to music itself. The score is a prayer book and she is a nun at her devotions. Her humility has the ferocity of revelation. For an instant, with almost mathematical precision, I feel that we are all arranged in a hierarchal pattern: the audience and the students beneath the singer, the singer beneath the miracle of music, and perhaps, because Ned O'Gorman is sitting next to me, by a kind of osmosis I sense a larger harmony above the whole.

At the close of the lesson Callas dismisses the pupils, tucks her scores under her arm, and, ignoring the ovation from the audience, moves quietly off the stage, her scarlet pajamas swaying with her stride, her long earrings dangling — a stylish school teacher, the day's work behind her.

Ned O'Gorman and I find ourselves outside again. It is already dark and by the light of the street lamps we can read the posters proclaiming tonight's opera with its cast.

CHAPTER X

Two Gothic Profiles

THE TALL IMPOSING FIGURES of T. S. Eliot and Pierre Teilhard de Chardin are linked in my mind. Their profiles, both with high bony noses like church buttresses, are etched into the future. Eliot was renowned during his own lifetime, but Teilhard de Chardin has grown famous since his death.

When I was at college Eliot was the poet above all others. Inside the mock Tudor campus buildings we sat in informal groups as our Marxist professors taught us from several bibles: *Das Kapital, Man's Fate, The Waste Land,* and *The Hollow Men.* Pseudo-leftists, uniformly dressed in pastel Brooks Brothers sweaters, fake pearl necklaces, and rubber-soled saddle shoes, we absorbed the poems line by line, convinced that *April is the cruelest month* or *This is the way the world ends/ Not with a bang but a whimper* were announcements of the fall of capitalist society. We were molded by our teachers from Monday to Friday. They pointed out to us with astonishing cheerfulness the approaching apocalypse, when they were not too busy listening to our private psychic problems. But at the weekend we returned to our bourgeois existences unaware that our minds were as piebald as our saddle shoes.

My interest in Eliot's poetry was revived by a reading he gave at the Y.M.H.A. in New York. The auditorium was filled to capacity: adolescent students of literature, writers, editors, critics, and fringe colleagues. They appeared eager but somewhat dusty, as though they had dwelt too long on dark library shelves. Sitting near us, two girls in blue jeans and striped sailor jerseys were vigorously chewing gum. Between snaps and clicks, one of them was saying, "It's not that I care about his poetry, I just want to get a look at him before he dies." This was cold reverence. But was it after all so different from my own image of him? I had not returned to Eliot since my college days but now that my husband had become his publisher I was eager to see the great man in the flesh. Tonight he was to read *The Waste Land*, the manifesto of my student days. He walked slowly from the dark wings across the lighted stage to the lectern. He was tall and angular as a Gothic cathedral, with that prominent nose, his eyes blinking in the sudden glare as sunken and lusterless as burned-out craters. His voice had organ tones, and soon the particulars of the man were lost in the poem itself: the agonized cries of the damned, the bereaved, the sage gazing too deeply into the abyss were interspersed by inane Cockney dialogue, crickets chirping in a graveyard. The political prophecy once disclosed to me by academic mentors was displaced by a vast lament, personal yet universal, more intelligible yet less explicit than the poem I had studied, all footnotes drowned in Eliot's resonant voice.

Phlebas the Phoenician, a fortnight dead,
Forgot the cry of gulls, and the deep sea swell
And the profit and loss.
     A current under sea
Picked his bones in whispers. As he rose and fell
He passed the stages of his age and youth
Entering the whirlpool.
      Gentile or Jew
O you who turn the wheel and look to windward,
Consider Phlebas, who was once handsome and tall as you

Later I read for the first time *Four Quartets* and *Ash Wednesday* and discovered the poet of formal religious quietude. The revolutionary spokesman for the "new generation" no longer existed, if he ever had. This grave voice was heard out of a timeless, unending metaphysical present.

During a visit to New York Eliot was staying with his friend and editor, Robert Giroux. As my husband and I entered Giroux's bachelor flat, my first impression of Eliot was again of size. His great stooping frame seemed to fill the small room. The large, gray, burned-out crater eyes looked surprisingly mild behind his glasses. He was pale; his features had a grandeur that made Giroux look rosy and round beside him. It would not have startled me if Eliot's natural voice had been a clap of thunder. Instead, he spoke with a clipped British accent about the difficulty of obtaining hotel accommodations in the Virgin Islands and about the spring climate in New York City.

"Bob and I sat in the sun in Central Park this afternoon," he said.

"Tom enjoyed watching the children playing," added Giroux, handing around the drinks and appetizers. Although the room still looked overcrowded, Eliot no longer seemed to be the cause. He sat comfortably ensconced on a black horsehair sofa, twirling his gold swizzle stick, a gift from an admirer, as he watched the champagne bubbles in his glass with the same expression of passive interest that I imagined he had shown while observing the children at play in the park.

We were going to the theater to see *My Fair Lady* because Cathleen Nesbitt was acting in it and she had starred in Eliot's *The Cocktail Party*. In the taxi there was a discussion as to whether he should go backstage to present his compliments before or after the performance. He was as nervous as any stagedoor Johnny. Bob Giroux listened, advised, encouraged, and with his help the decision was finally taken. He went afterward. As my turmoil at being with Eliot subsided, I observed with incredulity his mounting excitement, very much as mine had been at the prospect of meeting him.

After the theater we returned to Bob's apartment for a nightcap. The three men talked publishing, Eliot as senior member of Faber and Faber, the English firm. Now I saw him from a new angle: the London man of affairs. It was easy to picture him wearing the regulation bowler hat and chamois vest of the toiler in the City. My husband mentioned a volume of Turgenev reminiscences, never translated into English, that he was about to publish. I watched Eliot take a small pad from his pocket and scribble some notes. His long bony fingers handled the scrap of paper with dexterity, as though he were taking an order. The evening wore on and I managed to smother several yawns, feeling resentful that the T. S. Eliot I had looked forward to meeting had been so effectively concealed.

It was not until the next day that my husband realized that he had unwittingly presented Faber with an editorial acquisition, the unpublished reminiscences of Turgenev. And it was years and several meetings later before I was reconciled to the triviality of my Eliot encounters. I now believe that the vulnerable poet took refuge in the soothing hum of social chit-chat and shop talk just as crustaceans find protection inside the stuffy dark of a shell.

These days I read T. S. Eliot's poetry with increasing awe, but my image of him has become indistinct, as when the silvery disk of an autumnal sun is veiled by passing clouds in formations that imitate various earth species familiar to us below.

People often ask me, with wonder and envy combining in their voices, "Is it true that you actually knew Father Teilhard de Chardin?" I reply in the affirmative, yet I have no conviction that the man I remember is the same as the famous Jesuit philosopher, author of *The Human Phenomenon* and other books, creator of a system of thought whose purpose is the reconciliation of his two passionate loyalties: enduring Mother Church and that upstart ruler of this century, Science.

My first view of him antedates World War II. He was brought to our house one summer day by my cousin Rhoda, whose relationship with him, growing closer with the years, was to be my connection. They had met on a geological expedition some time before; now he was passing through the United States on his way to Peking for further paleontological work, a field in which he had already made important discoveries. He was in his late fifties, a tall aristocratic man in severe clerical black and white. His craggy head allowed one to divine the fine bones of his skull. His nose, high-bridged and aquiline, was reminiscent of Voltaire's. His eyes were especially compelling: small and deep-set, they were of indeterminate color, as though altered by the intensity of thought behind them. This Jesuit priest on his way to distant lands seemed to have no part in my life and I took note of him abstractly, the way one records the features of a passing landscape from the window of a moving train: a lonely farmhouse, a poplar-lined road, a solitary figure leaning on a rake in an open field — vivid, seen in detail for an instant before disappearing forever around a bend in the track.

Yet I was destined to meet Teilhard de Chardin again and often. Through the intricate design of chance, this French priest, after having been interned in China during the war years, was to make New York City his adopted home. And Rhoda, whose path had crossed his in Tibet, was to be his mainstay in exile for as long as he lived. He would be working for a science foundation here because the Catholic Church wanted him out of France, fearing his heretical philosophy that had already found a handful of ardent followers within the Order. But none of us was especially concerned with his ideas; we came to take him for granted as a type of benign and unobtrusive elderly uncle.

The album opens with a snapshot of him seated at the family board at one of the Sunday luncheon rituals at my father's apartment. My father, a recent widower, would gather stray relatives and friends for interminable midday feasts that left us drowsy and stuffed. I see a typical grouping around the enlarged table covered in white damask, where the gold and white English china and cut crystal glasses, used only for evening galas in my mother's day, were now squandered in bachelor negligence throughout the numerous courses of the midday meal. The guests might include Aunt Helen (a relative by appointment rather than consanguinity), my mother's lifelong friend — an ex-beauty with faded rose petal skin, porcelain-blue eyes, a disdainful mouth, and a frizzy *belle époque* bang. She was accompanied by her spinster daughter, who looked like a governess but preserved in regard to her mother the obedient and furtive attitude of a timid child. The family doctor came next, an early Hitler refugee, square and blond with a Heidelberg dueling scar marring his lower lip. He looked most natural when sampling beer, the produce of my family's business. Also included was Estelle Leibling, a vivacious friend of my father's, a well-known singing coach who had launched many Metropolitan Opera stars and looked like a retired performer herself; along with my husband was my brother and his current wife, the motion picture actress Linda Darnell. I see her in full opulent color, with wide rich brown eyes and flowing dark hair; having just arisen she was wearing a negligée that revealed a broad expanse of snowy white chest and the deep cleavage of her bosom like an alpine ravine. She would be sipping genteelly from a tall glass (pure gin), while waiting for a long distance call from Athens, Rome, or Istanbul concerning a film. Nestled in the capacious sculptured hollow between her neck and shoulder, the camera has caught her pet marmoset, as meager and mangy as his mistress is voluptuous and smooth. He seems to be surveying the assembled guests with fearful disapproving eyes.

Father Teilhard de Chardin might be found next to this exotic pair with the ballast of Rhoda on his other side. But habit, that strongest of sedatives, allowed him to accept them as well as the other guests, just as we grew accustomed to him as merely another member of the group. I no longer examined him with the interested scrutiny of our first meeting. His long black-clothed frame and his white clerical collar were as much a part of the scene as the colorful Chinese screen that had always stood, for no apparent reason, at right angles to the swinging pantry door that divided the dining room from the nether regions in my parents' home. As regularly as the striking of a grandfather's clock, before the demitasses had been served, Father Teilhard would rise from the table and disappear into my father's bedroom for his afternoon nap. Now I understand how inflexible routine steadied him in the intricate juggling of his philosophic thought and comforted him in exile against the loss of native land, his Jesuit dwelling in the rue Monsieur in Paris, and the far-flung field trips that he had grown too old to pursue.

In retrospect unbelievable, though natural enough at the time, were my Wednesday afternoon walks in Central Park with Father Teilhard de Chardin. Rhoda had the idea that it would be calming for him and useful for us for him to give us French conversation lessons, so with our tutor between us we would dawdle over the paths, breaking into English whenever we were too lazy to search for the correct word in French. How incongruous these outings appear now, as wasteful as using a priceless Han vase for a common cooking pot.

On fine afternoons we would go to the Zoo for tea. Here on the terrace, surrounded by cages, inhaling the stale pungent odor of captive animals, we would watch the seals, sleek as black silk thread flicking under and over the waters of their mini-ocean. Their hoarse calls were both threatening and forlorn. I have always disliked zoos, but it amused Father Teilhard to see the baboons pacing their prison cells, scratching, defecating, plucking amorously at one another. He regarded this scatological exhibition in much the same way as he saw *les noirs* in South Africa or the Untouchables in India, without compassion, as a scientist. "But one must take the long view . . . ," he would remonstrate. Focusing on the details of here and now was not for him. His deep keen eyes seemed to be apprehending the universe in vast evolutionary stretches of time invisible to the rest of us.

One afternoon as we were rising to leave the cafeteria, Father Teilhard dropped the breviary he was carrying and a small card fluttered out and landed on the cement at our feet. It was a picture of Jesus in crude color, like the one I used to examine in Tini's room in my childhood, flanked on her bureau by a faded palm and her rosary. The same mild effeminate face was framed by the spiky gold halo and the plump rosy heart was depicted on the outside like a weeping valentine. As Father Teilhard reached down to retrieve it, our eyes met and a dark flush spread over his face. I wonder, was that flush a symptom of the schism in his mind where the remote philosopher-scientist and the faithful Catholic, both sophisticated and primitive, were constantly seeking accord?

Our country house in Westchester was always pleasing to Father Teilhard de Chardin. He claimed that it reminded him of the home of his childhood, but I could never understand in what way the suburbs of New York City could resemble his ancestral acres in the austere mountains of Auvergne. His birthplace and his large, fanatically religious family, left forever when he entered the priesthood at seventeen, seemed very far from our casual house and sunny garden, close to encroaching throughways and the noisy intrusion of the county airport. At twilight on summer evenings when we sat outside after dinner, he would gaze at our sprawling roof and the giant pincushions of box hedge in the garden with the relaxed satisfaction of a returned traveler. On these visits to Sarosca Farm he would shed his black suit and clerical collar for a polo shirt and slacks, which he wore with a shade of shy vanity that reminded me of myself putting on my first long evening dress.

Sometime, when my husband and I pass a gas station, Esso, Texaco, or Mobil, its pumps like robots lining the route, we enjoy reminiscing about him and the rides we all used to take through the green, shady countryside. Rhoda, a tourist in reverse, would point out the sights of interest. "Look, Pierre," she would exclaim, "over there is a real American gas station!" And he would absent-mindedly answer, *"Très gentil,"* a phrase he often used to describe a person or a place, with that far-off expression in his intense eyes geared only to the "long view."

Father Teilhard was accepting of people and like T. S. Eliot enjoyed the warmth of their proximity, but he was no shepherd and he had no wish for a flock. He was engaged in the lonely battle of the mind and at Sarosca Farm he spent part of each day writing in the guest room, conventional with its leftover, unread novels and ruffled dressing table. His philosophical writings were banned by the Church and they were unread by us too, for we remained strangely incurious about his work. Once, when he was visiting us on the eve of a trip to South America, where he was to attend a scientific conference, the travel bureau called to inquire if he would say Mass on shipboard. When he picked up the telephone his voice sounded unusually harsh, and the flush I had noticed at the Zoo as he bent to retrieve the picture of Jesus spread over his features again: "I would rather not say Mass. I am very sorry." Later Rhoda persuaded him to change his mind, which he did, I suspect, more to please her than from any priestly desire.

Season after season, for six years, Father Teilhard de Chardin was with us like a kindly relative, and I saw him only once stripped of the familiar. It was a bleak and windy day, fall or early spring, I no longer remember. The old elm at the end of the garden was bare, its black branches gesticulating widely in the gale. In the sky, clouds were churning. Through the French windows, frail protection against the onslaught, suddenly I saw a tall figure, black coattails flapping, a supernatural apparition with an open prayer book held in long Gothic hands — a pious scarecrow circling the house. Like the elm, it seemed conjured from the elements, untamed as the wind itself, dark as the storm-tossed sky. It was a moment before I identified Father Teilhard de Chardin, and then, swiftly as though I had been eavesdropping, before he should notice me I moved to another part of the house.

One other incident has since appeared significant, an intimation of things to come. We were lunching at the country club where my husband and I played tennis and swam in the summer. It was off season and, stripped of its outdoor uses, the monster clubhouse, like a resort hotel from the twenties, was a blot on the landscape. The four of us were seated at a table near a window overlooking the golf course, dotted sparsely with a few hardy players muffled up against the cold. The big dining hall was overheated and over-decorated with gilded columns and wainscoting. The club membership includes many Irish Catholics, and this day saw the usual complement of fat, well-fed priests. Father Teilhard, though wearing the same habit, looked a breed apart, with his narrow head, his penetrating eyes, and his cultivated, slightly French accent. He was like a princely guest in the plush and gold drawing room of the nouveaux riches. Perhaps moved by his unselfconscious superiority, I had an unusual impulse to talk to him about his writing. "How do you have the patience to go on?" I asked. "The Church has muzzled you. Will you ever be published if you remain a part of it?" I had heard from Rhoda about his endless and unavailing appeals to the Vatican.

"It is no matter," Father Teilhard answered, "my thought is for the Church. Outside, I could no longer serve it. I am confident that Catholicism will go my way. If I am instrumental, good; if not, I am content to be a drop in the sea. The essential is that what I believe will prevail in the end."

He looked directly at me, then down at his neglected fruit cup and abruptly changed the subject, but not before I had caught a spark illuminating something rare in our midst. And this dedication would have its reward, for almost immediately following his death in the fifties his books were released and acclaimed by the world, within as well as outside the Church.

On my walks over the city I like to peer into bookshop windows. In recent years I often find the works of Teilhard de Chardin piled up like pyramidal bricks. I am always confronted by the same display photograph of the author. His cheeks are hollow, his features have architectural proportions, and I strain in vain to uncover the human being in this formal black and white representation. The store window is shallow and a mirror panel reveals merely my own image in passing reflection. I must shore up the past against oblivion. I must place my scraps of recollection of Teilhard de Chardin before the altar remains of a skeletal cathedral.

CHAPTER XI

The Road to Mandalay

AT FIRST GLANCE the picture on the card appeared to be Cape Cod. This was to be expected, because it was summer, when my post office box often contains greetings from some beach where refugees from the city stretched out in the sun, oiled and relaxed, are overtaken by a day of rain and, confined to a sandy cottage, are reduced to writing friends back home. On second glance, the jut of land into the blatant blue water looked foreign. I turned the card over and read: "Tomorrow Peking!" The signature: "Dinah and Jimmy." I noted the Hong Kong stamp and I understood that the Sheeans, so many years later, were once more on the road to where the action was most intense, having fled their retreat on a lake in northern Italy.

Sometimes people can be recalled most clearly after they have been removed by death or geographical distance. Some insignificant object, sight, sound, or smell is empowered to return them more vividly than those we encounter each day. The Sheeans have become part of this company. Their paths no longer cross mine. During many years we met by accident or by design, and yet, although they were certainly a most dramatic, handsome couple, for some reason the early days of our acquaintance made little impression on me. During World War II they were correspondents in the old-fashioned romantic style. Together they covered the Spanish Civil War, burning for a cause, charging their courage to the very limits of their personal strength. James Vincent Sheean had been everywhere: recording the London blitz, the Italian, French, North African theaters of war, the Pacific. Before our meeting, his best-selling memoir, *Personal History*, his view of the already legendary early days of Communism in China and Russia in the 1920s and 30s, had been published.

My initial introduction to the Sheeans has been mislaid in a haze of forgetfulness. I do remember one scene from that period because of its oddness. It is like a dream recalled in minute detail, and like a dream it is apparently senseless. The setting is my mother-in-law's town house, the time is mid-morning soon after the end of World War II. I see a gathering in the stately drawing room which is complete with conservatory, velvet upholstery, and damask drapes. But the actors appear to be featureless; only the Sheeans, the leads, are rescued from this erasure. He is tall, with a fair boyish face although he is already in his forties. She, some fifteen years younger (my age), a beauty, has long wild black hair, clear blue eyes, and high color. She reminds me of a heroine from an English novel, an apparition blown into the house on East Ninety-third Street from some windy moor. But, strangely, she is wearing a loose floor-length velvet gown that looks as though it had been retrieved from the wardrobe trunk of her famous Shakespearean actor parents: Sir Johnston Forbes-Robertson and Gertrude Elliott. The plot of the improbable dream revolves around the fire in Dorothy Thompson's Bronxville villa where the Sheeans have been living with their two small daughters. I had seen its false Tudor complacency, so unsuited to this couple returned from their passionate far-flung adventures. In my mind's eye it appeared as though two flames had been trapped inside a cardboard doll's house and had demolished it in angry conflagration. All had escaped. But what were they doing here surrounded by this faceless group? And why were my husband and I included? True, Jimmy Sheean had been a long-standing friend of my mother-in-law's, and my husband and Dinah had together compiled a book of war letters from Britain. But was this a rescue committee, a social gathering, a charitable event? As in a dream the scene persists in meaninglessness. Only the details are telling, and Dinah's crumpled emerald-green velvet robe worn at mid-morning appears, in retrospect, like a flag signaling sudden danger and disaster. The play is without beginning or end and I did not see the Sheeans again for a long time, nor do I remember giving any thought to them during those years.

The next appearance of Vincent Sheean causes me to wonder at my blindness. One's attention is like a lighthouse illuminated by the imagination, which revolves to reveal a section of landscape here, a figure there, leaving all else in comparative darkness. It was at Marlboro College, at that same writers' conference where I had focused so exclusively on Charles Jackson, that Vincent Sheean appeared again — but as far as I was concerned, he played only a walk-on part.

At that time he was living in nearby Vermont, alone, as he and Dinah had been divorced. He was guest speaker at the symposium and I recall his entrance into the auditorium out of a dark sultry rainy night. He looked the perfect prototype of foreign correspondent in a dripping trench coat, collar turned up, belted, with something swashbuckling and romantic about his appearance — but solitary, as though the many sights he had seen, the miles he had traveled had been seen and traveled alone. I remember nothing of his lecture, and although my husband and I talked with him afterwards, no word of the conversation is recorded in my memory. But I did observe that his face had remained boyish, though his fair hair was turning gray and receding to reveal the high domed forehead of a prophet. His small blue eyes were penetrating but looked pained, and he squinted as though he were staring into a hurtful sun.

Why was I so neglectful of him that evening when later he was to be of so much interest? What caused the small comical figure of Charles Jackson to present itself instead as a valuable discovery? These selections, seemingly so capricious and mysterious, are, I suppose, based on subconscious needs that alter and disappear.

There was another lapse of years and Dinah Sheean telephoned to invite us for dinner. She and Jimmy had been remarried but were living separately in New York apartments. Hers, in the Murray Hill area, was cluttered with murky Victorian portraits, memorabilia of her famous actor parents and their cohorts, and stacks of books, papers, a typewriter — evidence of her own work. The room had a slovenly aspect like a bohemian eccentric. Dinah was more at home on the road than contained in a mold of domesticity. But her enthusiasm and responsiveness provided a hearth. She was still handsome, but the long free black hair had been tamed into a cropped head of crisp graying curls, and she had grown heavier. Her clear blue eyes and high color remained unchanged as well as her beautiful contralto voice and faultless English.

"Jimmy is coming for dinner," she said as though honoring us with a deity. In spite of the ups and downs of their relationship, the separations, battles, and disappointments, she had managed to preserve some of the image of the adventurous, idealistic writer she had married, who for her would always retain a touch of genius.

When Jimmy arrived I was startled to see that he was old. The reaction was a subjective one. It is always a shock after the passage of years to realize that people are not frozen into the age when last seen but have moved inexorably along an escalator, and to realize that we are moving too. A lapse in time uncovers buried thoughts; it is the skeleton at the spectacle. Jimmy had grown portly, he had a paunch, and his nose was gross and covered with a network of red, the map of years of hard drinking. The fringe surrounding his high forehead was white, he stooped and shuffled. But his greeting had the remembered hint of midwestern twang under its layer of declamatory theatricality.

The evening proceeded in a friendly unremarkable way, interspersed with the do-you-remembers of long acquaintanceship. As usual the dialogue has vanished; only pictures remain. For this reason, there is no logical path to my tardy discovery of Vincent Sheean, nor do I know a specific reason for it. After dinner, Dinah, my husband and I, and an anonymous couple were grouped at one side of the room and Jimmy in a rocker was opposite us. All at once, he seemed to be transformed, to tower, threatening the intimate scene. He was in profile to me: I see his domed forehead, one hand with long tapering fingers raised in prophetic gesture. Here was someone worth studying, although I sensed that for me he would always remain elusive, a puzzle. Then and there I determined to read every one of his books, to find him in them and to recover, as much as possible, lost time.

It is accurate to state that I came to know Vincent Sheean through his works and that our meetings during the years when we were neighbors in New York City did little to detract from that relationship. I began with the rereading of *Personal History;* why had I previously been untouched by the conflict between the questing idealist and the hedonist addicted to luxurious living, seduced by the spurious glitter of the very wealthy and the worldly famous? I continued with *Not Peace but a Sword* (on the Spanish Civil War) and his World War II memoirs: *Between the Thunder and the Sun* and *This House Against This House.* I devoured them without interruption. Recognition through literature may cause the heart to pound like love, it is as rare and, in its way, as mysterious, never based solely on abstract merit. Why did these books come to mean so much to me, so late, after the events described in them had passed on into history? Why had I overlooked them when they were in vogue? Some chance granted me the privilege of reading them together; the works of an author depend upon one another, enhancing each other so that even the flaws and eccentricities become attractive and we wholeheartedly assume their obsessions as our own. In his books Vincent Sheean reveals two selves equally: the poet-dreamer and the man of action, a dichotomy especially attractive to me. He possesses a lyrical identification with place and there is almost no corner of the earth that has not imprinted itself on his sensibility — and I cannot help feeling that, in return, his intense vision has left an enduring impression in its wake.

Perhaps the man of action in Sheean's war books appeals to me because my view of the war had been so sequestered, self-centered, concentrated on those close to me, while his ranged far and wide, motivated by a patriotism I have never experienced. Despite his keen intelligence he reveals himself to be more idealistic and intuitive than analytical. His words throw open a thrilling world. For this, long after the events described, I thanked him. I followed these books with his biographies and memoirs of other people: his delicate, sentient portrait of Edna St. Vincent Millay, the more intimate and probing recollections of Dorothy Thompson and Sinclair Lewis, the biographies of Verdi and Gandhi — the latter somewhat superficial, not altogether successful, but disclosing the mystical side of Sheean, a kind of Irish-American guru with alternating qualities of susceptibility and detachment. His attitude to the Mahatma is filial, worshipful; he had arrived from Vermont to sit at the "Bapus'" feet for life, he believed on the very day of the assassination. What novelist can compete with the peculiar dramatic coincidences that certain lives attract? Finally I came to the book I was to reread most frequently, *First and Last Love*, the chronicle of Sheean's lifelong love affair with music. It began during his childhood in Pana, Illinois, grew during his college years at the University of Chicago, flourished with the rise of his career as foreign correspondent, and continues to this very day. He has been ardently present at every opera house and concert hall in the world. In spite of his thorough self-taught knowledge of music, he is awed and shy in the presence of virtuosos. I have often heard him exclaim, "In my next reincarnation I want to be an opera singer!"

I am persuaded that his wish may be granted because there is an uncanny identification between him and my own joy in music, especially opera. When I listen to Verdi's *Falstaff*, Jimmy is there. The bravura, the blustery passions, the bawdy comedy, clownishness, delicate tenderness, and the melancholy of Verdi's sublime music characterizing Shakespeare's aging, fat, tipsy courtier do not so much remind me of Jimmy as return him with supernatural immediacy. Far away, mostly forgotten and unbidden, he is conjured up, more real than when we were actually sitting side by side at the dinner table long ago.

For several years he lived three blocks from us across Third Avenue. New York divides itself into numerous residential sections, small villages within its vastness. So I would frequently run into Jimmy in our neighborhood and we would hail one another with the familiarity of fellow visitors on the esplanade of some spa or seaside resort. But we were environed by jerry-built apartment buildings, cafeterias, bars, laundromats, and supermarkets. As I watched him approach he would seem out of place, the world traveler grounded here. He was a little shabby and would sometimes be wearing a blue beret reminiscent of Montparnasse or Trastevere. It looked insignificant perched at a jaunty angle atop his large Churchillian head. He used a cane with swagger and I never could decide whether it was ornament or necessity. His walk was slightly pigeon-toed, vaguely pathetic, childlike. But the bulk and height of his frame were impressive — yet sad, too — he reminded me of one of those huge ocean liners docked in a Hudson pier and now used only for Caribbean cruises when once it had constituted the sole means of crossing the great Atlantic Ocean. Our greeting would be banal and we would move on in our differing directions. But at odd hours, often late at night, he would call — I suspect, drunk. He used his friends to expound, on the telephone, his rage and grief at the way the world was going: the Vietnam war, the Israelis and the Arabs, the plight of the blacks — and over all, his shame and pride, his love and hatred of his own country and his identification with its guilt.

It was difficult to lure him to our house, out of his lair. I had never been inside that lair, but I pictured it crammed with books and his beloved records and he had told me that it overlooked Manhattan House. I imagine that this view into the abodes of the very rich was not displeasing to him! It is my belief that at this period the crossing of Third Avenue was more of an enterprise for Jimmy than his occasional trips to Saudi Arabia to visit King Faisal in connection with a book he was then working on. Space, like time, is comparative, subject to state of mind, and in certain moods three city blocks can stretch as wide as the world.

When he did arrive for dinner he was often high, uproarious, outrageous, with that brand of humor that is the other side of sadness. I recall one evening in particular when he and Joe Liebling composed ad lib dirty limericks on (of all subjects) Willa Cather — while Jean Stafford, Liebling's wife, and my husband and I implored them to stop to allow us to regain our breath and ease our aching ribs. But they went on, irrepressible, inexhaustible, and the limericks proliferated into the small hours of the morning. At other times, Jimmy, always a profuse name-dropper, would compose cables of warning, congratulations, condolence, advice, or salutation to such varied characters as Winston Churchill, Nehru, Eleanor Roosevelt, Martin Luther King, Lady Diana Duff-Cooper, Golda Meir, or Leontyne Price.

Once or twice during the summer my husband and I would coax him out of his hibernation for a weekend at our house in the country. But it was never a success. He squinted at the trees as though they were hostile, and I do not believe that suburban family life had ever been a congenial environment for Jimmy. After we returned him in front of his apartment canopy I saw him disappear inside the welcoming obscurity of his own lobby like a great bear released from behind the bars of a zoo into his native forest.

The elegance of formal dinner parties was more attractive to him. He was able to kindle to evening attire, jewels, expensive wine. When I went with him to the new opera house at Lincoln Center we would dress with the pomp of visiting royalty, although, much to his disgust, we might be surrounded by blue jeans and matted, lank, androgynous locks. But *Die Walküre, Tosca,* or *La Traviata* were cure-alls. They formed an enduring bridge spanning past and present, a recourse when all else failed.

After reading Henri Troyat's biography of Leo Tolstoy, I devoted a winter to the reading and rereading of that writer exclusively, in much the same way as I had immersed myself in the books of Vincent Sheean. To crown my Tolstoy season Jimmy decided that I must visit his old friend,

Alexandra Tolstoy (youngest daughter of the author), at the emigré commune she founded at Blauveldt on the Hudson.

The time came in early March, a Sunday: Jimmy warned us that we would have to attend the Orthodox service at the community church and that we would be obliged, according to custom, to remain standing throughout the long ceremony. It was a muggy day and the air was as oppressive as a saturated blanket. It was too soon for signs of spring, and as the four of us — my husband and I, Jimmy and Dinah — moved along the parkway the country was drained of all color. There was no hint or promise of the season to come. Barren trees, earth, sky were etched in gray, brown, and black, submissive to the steady downpour. As my husband drove, the windshield wipers hummed and we were rather silent, even Jimmy, as though we were conserving our energy for the strain of the service we were about to attend.

The church was small, onion-domed, oddly alien set down on New York State farmland. Within it was dark, stifling, and crowded. Through the obscurity I made out that the worshipers were all elderly or ancient, the last relics of the Czarist regime. The men — in the minority — wore frayed dark suits that had seen better days; the women were shrouded in drab shawls and looked like old-time immigrants huddled at Ellis Island. The ritual was endless, incomprehensible to me, and after a while I felt myself swaying on my feet. My husband and Dinah looked exhausted and restless too — only Jimmy stood erect, his eyes fixed straight ahead to the altar with its icons and flickering candles.

At the close of the ceremony the old people filed outside in a slow march, huddled under dripping black umbrellas.

Suddenly Jimmy, breaking rank, rushed forward and stopped before the figure of a diminutive shawled woman. Bowing low, in courtier style, he raised her shriveled hand to his lips and kissed it, murmuring reverently the name of Countess Tolstoy. I shall never forget the expression on the woman's wrinkled face: a combination of incredulity and coquetry. How long had it been since a gallant courtier had bowed over her hand? At that moment no plumed hat, satin breeches, or decorations could have rendered Jimmy more aristocratic, and the drab woolen shawl might have been part of a sweeping court ball gown. But the error was soon revealed: it was not Alexandra Tolstoy, but an anonymous member of her flock. Jimmy blushed when he discovered his mistake but it was evident that he had given to the homesick transplanted little old woman a moment of intense unexpected joy — a whiff of olden days lost in the new country, a brief return of her own vanished prestige. It was explained that Countess Tolstoy had not attended the service and that we would find her at her cottage where she was awaiting us.

When we were ushered into her presence I experienced a shock. Here, lacking only the flowing beard, was the old Tolstoy himself. The resemblance between father and daughter was uncanny. She was a hulking woman in her eighties but strong and vigorous, with her father's small intelligent eyes, his wide turnip nose, and his imposing head which had something Jovian about its proportions.

Jimmy, recovered from his mistake, was soon at ease with his "old friend." We had a plentiful but coarse lunch with Countess Tolstoy in the common dining hall, while she explained the operation of the commune, its self-sufficiency, and its perpetuation. When I took stock of the average age, the latter seemed dubious. It would not be long before they would all vanish beneath the ground of the cemetery in the lee of the small onion-domed church. Alexandra Tolstoy herself was an anachronism, although a flourishing one who looked as though she might live forever. She ate like a *mujik* and was violent in her denunciation of Communists. Her attitude indicated that it would not surprise her to find one lurking beneath each dining hall table. And her forceful muscular person convinced me that she would be able to roll up her sleeves and deal effectively by herself with each enemy. Jimmy mentioned my reading of the Troyat biography. "Ugh! a disgusting book! It should never have been allowed publication. What an ugly, lying portrait of my father!" she replied. Although I did not agree with her I could understand her recoil. The intimate diaries of her parents, exhibited for all the world to see, were a public undressing, and I was aware that my interest in the book was in part a kind of keyhole peeping at the great. It was obvious that to Alexandra Tolstoy, still her father's ardent disciple, he had been defamed. Strangers should know him through his work alone.

Returned to her living quarters, we were introduced to her partner. She was younger than Countess Tolstoy and it was obvious that their relationship was scratchy and competitive. She looked like any headmistress of a boarding school. It was explained that she had not joined us at lunch as she was recovering from the flu. The conversation grew dull and I amused myself by examining the collection of old family photographs that had been smuggled out of Russia. The pictures of Tolstoy's wife and sister as young women attracted me in particular. Both were brunette, pretty, and pert (so different from the masculine ponderous daughter of Tolstoy), and I knew that the blending of these two had produced the character of Natasha in *War and Peace*. As my attention returned to the conversation around me, my husband was asking Alexandra Tolstoy how she felt about accepting the donation of money recently received from Stalin's daughter, Svetlana. Countess Tolstoy was silent for a moment. Her small gray eyes were thoughtful, then twinkled as she answered with a shrug and a sigh of pious resignation, "It was God's will!" For me the day was made. The expression in those eyes, that response! I had not only met the daughter — here was Lev Tolstoy himself come to life again. For this opportunity I felt an impulse of gratitude to Jimmy.

Later Countess Tolstoy conducted us over the muddy saturated ground of her vegetable garden. She tended it herself and I could picture her digging and hoeing. I examined her strong, callused, gnarled hands and felt certain that the produce she cultivated must be as hardy and perennial as she was herself. In parting she presented my husband with some of her tomato seeds in a small paper packet which she skillfully folded. They flourish in our garden today — large bursting red vegetable flesh — they connect our place, like widely separated kin, with Yasnaya Polyana.

Jimmy's disgust with the United States grew in proportion to his age and the slowing down of his writing activities. He continued to pay periodic visits to King Faisal and I'm certain that royal hospitality extended from any quarter of the globe could still warm the cockles of his heart. But he talked more and more about leaving his country forever.

"I plan to die in Rome," he would say. I could not help feeling that there was something operatic in his choice — a final *addio* from the Eternal City. In spite of his sixty-odd years and poor health it was easier to believe in his living than in his dying. His obsession with his demise was like an assurance, a knocking on wood, and his boisterous gallows humor, never far from an awareness of the fleeting human condition, showed a respectful attitude to the enemy's strength. It was a defense. While others, busy and unheeding, would be suddenly felled, Jimmy would survive. So I believed, and also so wished.

True to his plan, in preparation, he moved to Rome. His tall Churchillian presence was seen no more on Third Avenue. On an autumn visit to Rome my husband and I telephoned him at the *pensione* where he was staying. His familiar voice, midwestern, slightly theatrical, spanned the months since we had met.

My husband and I strolled toward the Borghese Gardens on the way to Jimmy's *pensione*. The street was crowded, lined on both sides by little café tables and chairs set out in the sunshine. The mob was as dense as at a carnival. Pimps, prostitutes, the over-rich, the over-poor, jostled one another, staring and commenting like the audience at a freak show. But who was audience and who was freak? It was impossible to say. Straight ahead the dark gray ancient Aurelian Wall bordering the park seemed to be surveying the jostling hordes with the composure and serenity of a sage comparing the absurdity of frail humanity with the solidity and endurance of stone. The Park was as lush as midsummer, dark green, with venerable trees providing shade like cool water. Surrounding the Villa Borghese there was a clearing of gravel paths

and formal gardens, planted with zinnias and chrysanthemums. They drooped and looked dusty like a straggling
remnant of the retinue that had once guarded the palace
of the proud princes of the Renaissance, now thrown open
to the public as a museum.

Jimmy's dwelling, Pensione Villa Borghese, was located
outside the Gardens opposite the palace. It was shabby
and inconspicuous and we were ushered into the salon, a
small underfurnished room that reminded me of the visitors'
parlor of a school. The ill-assorted chairs were uncomfortable, there was a rickety television set, and on the coffee
table a vase of wilting pink carnations attempted in vain to
add a touch of cheer. The landlady left to announce our
presence, and Jimmy soon arrived in crumpled army khakis.
He looked as though we had roused him from a nap. Although he appeared cheerful, a little jaunty, his mood
failed. His cheer was as unavailing as the pink carnations
on the coffee table that separated us. We talked of home,
of the bad state of things, of mutual friends, but I had no
impression of his life in Rome, except for his saying, "Every
afternoon I visit the Princess Paulina across the street at
the Villa Borghese." When we rose to leave, Jimmy in his
creased army attire became as ceremonious as an emperor.
Every farewell was, after all, perhaps the final one.

Walking back to our hotel I felt oppressed. While my
husband went on I decided to visit the Borghese Palace. It
was cool and dark inside with a musty smell common to all
museums. I inquired of a guard the direction to Canova's
famous statue of Napoleon's sister, Paulina. I found her
stretched out on her marble couch, her white marble draperies falling away to disclose the perfection of her white marble

body, seductive but cold. One white marble tendril escaped coyly from her white marble coiffure. So this was Jimmy's royal friend, companion to lonely ex-patriotism. Suddenly the room had the clamminess of death and the body stretched on the couch became a corpse. I hurried away into the warm sunshine, propelled by a wave of overwhelming homesickness.

Jimmy did not remain in Rome. The site chosen for his demise was discarded after all. He made several sorties back to New York City but they were, apparently, failures too. On his last visit he stayed at Dinah's empty apartment. She was in Paris accompanied by Charlie, her fiercely loyal black cocker spaniel. He was always near her like a small black shadow. She was deep in endless research for a biography of a forgotten French hero of the Revolution who had died young in Napoleon's army. Jimmy commented on this project, "It's no book, it's a way of life!" I had heard her speak of "Aristide" with characteristic verve and admiration. It occurred to me that her impression of the idealistic French soldier, long dead, might somewhat resemble the Vincent Sheean she had known and loved; her collaborator during the months of the Spanish Civil War, now grown as historic as the French Revolution.

Several years ago, in late spring Jimmy finally left the United States to live abroad. We said goodbye in a city restaurant, my husband and I not wanting to subject him again to the hostility of the trees at our country place. We waited at the bar long past the appointed hour and were about ready to give up and go home when he appeared, huge and wavering, already monstrously drunk. We squeezed ourselves around a table in the crowded room, my husband and

I on the banquette against the wall, Jimmy opposite us. He was very red in the face and his eyes squinted in that pained way as though the dark restaurant reflected a hurtful sun. He drank copiously and continuously, eating nothing, toying with the expensive food on his overfilled plate. His dialogue ranged widely, incoherently, the flashes of his keen intellect and humor almost, but not completely, obliterated by alcohol. Periodically, there would be a significant silence after which he would roar, "Tell me, do you think I should marry Indira Gandhi?" The reiterated question became a leitmotif, involuntarily shared by our fellow diners. I wished the long dinner would end but kept wondering how we would ever achieve our exit with Jimmy. Once he leaned toward us across the table and stated firmly and clearly, with sudden sobriety, "It's strange, I had been looking forward to this evening and it has turned out to be nothing at all." He had uttered my unspoken thought with uncanny precision. We finally managed to maneuver him out, dropped him at Dinah's door, and drove back to the country.

I have not seen him since. He settled on Lago Maggiore, a final retreat, protected by distant snow-capped Alps, a more impregnable terrain than Third Avenue or the Borghese Gardens. And Dinah joined him there; they were reunited once again, this time, I believe, for good. Dinah is a miraculous letter writer, and wherever she happens to be she can make place and people spring to life. So I can see the apartment over a grocery store where they live with Bill, a pug, the successor to Charlie. She never complains, but I sense her confinement in their small roost. She writes buoyantly that now that Jimmy has achieved the seventies, having outlived and defeated the changeling sixties, he has become a Grand Old Man. She is stubborn in her faith that his best book is still to come. She writes about their trips to Milan to La Scala and his renewal in opera which she shares. But I have my own picture of him. It is evening and he is on his way to what he calls "his lake," revived by a visit to the local pub. He walks in that slightly pigeon-toed childish fashion and he is wearing the old blue beret. He sits on a bench under the stars gazing across the still water and talks, talks endlessly to his captive audience, the village mayor. He discourses in fluent Italian, but sometimes interjects phrases in English, French, or German like trophies from his years of travel. He quotes Shakespeare, Dante, Croce, switching effortlessly from philosophy to politics, to literature, to music. His uproarious gallows humor and his mysterious insight are like flares illuminating the stagnant lake. Night after night the mayor listens submissively, marveling at the crazy American *signor*. Now and then Jimmy pays a visit to the town post office and sends off one of his bombastic cables to President Nixon, Indira Gandhi, or Golda Meir.

I had thought that this was the closing chapter of Jimmy's life until I received the card with its short rousing message: "Tomorrow Peking!" It was like a battle cry holding Time and its destructive army at bay. Here was no dwindling off into the wavering traceries of old age — instead, a bold line was curving around to form a complete circle.

CHAPTER XII

The Beauty

IT IS APPROPRIATE that my earliest views of my cousin Iris were photographs. A mirror image might have told her story even better, but it would have required her corporeal presence and at that time I had not yet met her. One picture shows her as a bridesmaid to my mother, the bride — the other, in reverse, but of the same vintage, as they were married six months apart. The brides are wearing yards of tulle veiling; each bridesmaid is crowned with a wreath of white flowers. Both women are lovely, my mother ethereal, Iris curved and voluptuous. Yet although my mother's image is the more perfect, Iris's reputation is firmly attached to hers and I see her through the lens of opinion. She is The Beauty and she will hold that title as long as she lives.

Though only five years her junior, she was my mother's niece, daughter of her oldest sister. It had been a family of six girls, two having died in infancy, and a brother, the only son, who died at twenty-one. My mother and Iris grew up together in the same high-stooped brownstone in New

York City; Iris's father, a business failure, had been given shelter and employment by his father-in-law, my grandfather. The older sisters were beautiful also, exotic, tinged by nervous maladies and hushed-up indiscretions. They were like orchids raised under glass in a hothouse, and I visualize the whole family, in semi-mourning for the lost son and brother, painted in shades of gray, white, mauve, and purple. My mother and Iris, the youngest, struggled for air in this atmosphere, growing closer than sisters, more congenial than chosen friends.

When Iris, who lived in California, did enter my life, I marveled at her intimacy with my mother, so unlike did they appear. My unworldly mother wore the dowdy clothes of a governess, and her graying ash-blond hair was dressed in an unfashionable bun and crimped by a scarecrow who came to the house with her implements: a curling iron and an alcohol lamp extracted from a black satchel that looked as though it belonged to a horse-and-buggy doctor. Iris, on the other hand, was impeccable, her clothes came from Paris and her golden hair was twisted into an intricate Grecian coiffure. The proportions of her body were classical too, her carriage poised, queenly, the result of daily exercises performed like rituals. What is there to say now of her beauty except that it was not true beauty but a form of art — which is, perhaps, the truer after all. Her skin was milky, no ray of sun ever touched her face, which was shaded in summer under the brim of a picture hat. Her eyes were blue-gray, the color of denim — but such homely texture could not be associated with Iris — rather, they were like sapphires that had been crossed with the cloudiness of opals. Her nose was aristocratic, with long narrow nostrils lined in pink like the mother-of-pearl interior of a shell; her mouth full-lipped, slightly asymmetrical, sensuous but controlled, was an instrument made especially to project her musical speech, a cool caress.

There are people who remain in memory inseparable from their dwellings; Iris was one of these. The luxury of her perfumed presence will always be linked in my mind with her country home on the outskirts of San Francisco. The smell of eucalyptus trees, the lush lawns moistened by the diamond-faceted arcs of sprinklers, the ivy-smothered house — all partake of Iris and she of them. Like its mistress the place was not precisely beautiful but it presented itself to me as a veritable Eden: tropical gardens outside, and inside, deep-cushioned flowered chintz sofas, huge Oriental porcelain bowls filled with heavy-headed pink peonies, and fresh figs in cream for breakfast. This Eden was ruled by a mythical goddess, a Venus, who gracefully descended to us from her private bower above.

On my first visit to Burlingame when I was about eight, I lived with my family in the bungalow usually occupied by Iris's mother-in-law. It was a satellite to the big house, and it was lined throughout with gold wallpaper. In the morning when I awoke I would often see from my window my cousin Manfred, a year younger than I, playing with his sailboat around the lily pond. In the fresh early light he was an angelic vision in patched corduroys, another emanation from Iris, his tousled blond curls as luxuriant as the peony petals; he had his mother's large deep-shadowed gray-blue eyes and her milky skin. But he lopes uncertainly into memory on coltish legs while she floats grandly as a swan.

The days of the summers at Burlingame were so alike that

they merge into one endless day — always sunlit, the nights cool, redolent of the eucalyptus trees. With my brother and my cousins Manfred and Marian, I would be caught in random holiday preoccupations, but Iris's time was ordered, a serene backdrop for our tumbled hours. She always remained in her bedroom until late, rarely emerging before noon. The perfection of her appearance made one think that she had devoted the morning hours to her mirror, an artist working at her easel. Occasionally when we were living in the big house I would catch a glimpse of Iris breakfasting in bed. She would be wearing a white silk Japanese kimono: we had similar ones, Marian's pale pink, mine jade green, and we looked like handmaidens to the deity. But my mother wore her flannel wrapper. Without make-up in the early morning, Iris, though lovely, looked slightly faded, her fine skin papery, her blue-gray eyes paler, set in darker shadows. Only her cushioned, well-tended hands, with tapered fingers topped by long, pointed, pink-enameled nails, and the white, rounded smoothness of her forearms, revealed as the kimono sleeves slid back while she sipped her aromatic morning tea, seemed already prepared for public appearance. My mother, on the contrary, in the old blue wrapper with her open hair falling to her waist, was at her best before the day began. If Iris, when composed, was a painting — a formal fête champêtre by Watteau — my mother's beauty had the simplicity of sculpture, perfect modeling of bone showing through transparent skin which defied all artifice and decoration.

Every afternoon at five exactly, Iris crossed the gravel path to pay a ritual call on her mother-in-law, Juliet, who lived in the bungalow with her spinster sister, Portia. The incongruity of those names strikes me now. Then I took for granted that an ancient white-haired rosy-cheeked lady should bear the name of Juliet, while her companion, sere and swarthy, shrill as a parakeet, should be called Portia — and that these two should dwell snugly in a golden-papered cottage. It was all part of a familiar fairy tale as taken for granted as "Hansel and Gretel" or "Little Red Riding Hood." But there was nothing of the fable in Iris's inflexible sense of duty. Her appearance on the walk between the houses was as regular as a clock's strike. Her perfect body, held so straight, cast its shadow over the lush lawn with the rectitude of a sundial indicating the hour.

At night Iris glowed. In the living room we awaited her descent. She arrived in clouds of chiffon draperies, enveloping all of us in her special scent. After dinner we would lounge in the softness of chintz sofas while only Iris sat erect, never allowing her back to graze the tempting cushions. After a day in each other's company, she and my mother talked on as though there were no bottom to the depth of their intimacy. At these times my father and Iris's husband remained in the background, shadows in memory.

One day when the adults had gone off somewhere in the car, Marian, Manfred, my brother, and I decided to build a tree house. The gardener provided us with planks and helped us place the platform in a crook of branches, high up. We took turns surveying our realm from this lookout — with the exception of my brother, unnaturally tall and gawky, who shouted instructions from below, attempting to transform fear into command. I too, although I did not admit it, preferred observing on terra firma. The grass, a violent green, sparkled with artificial dew and looked all the brighter because I was aware that outside the gate the hills were bare, parched brown. The palm trees rattled in the breeze, in the vegetable garden the tomatoes were ripening, golden red, and I could smell their fragrance from afar. A dragon fly darted in and out of the flower beds, teasing the petals with its tiny, whirring thrust. A yellow and black butterfly halted for an instant on a giant mauve zinnia, as though it were seated on a boudoir *pouffe*, contemplating its own beauty reflected many times over in the beauty of the garden — its existence paralleled by the perfection of the summer moment before it flew away.

It was Manfred's turn to climb into the tree house. I watched his patched corduroys ascending until his curly head merged with the leaves. Standing on the board he waved to us below and then there was a cracking sound as one of the planks broke loose. Manfred came tumbling down, the fall rendered in slow motion to the thick thudding of my heart. He hit the ground at last, landing flat on his back, his upturned face registering only mild surprise before he lost consciousness. We rushed for help, the gardener and the maids from the house seeming to form a mob scene. Manfred, as if dead, was carried inside. An ambulance broke the spell of the sunny garden; an invading army, it left horror in its wake. Marian, my brother, and I awaited the return of our parents, Marian having been delegated to break the news.

At last the car turned into the driveway, and before it could reach the house we signaled like hitchhikers for it to stop. Everyone got out. I remember noting irrelevantly that Iris was wearing a pale peach silk shirtwaist dress with her monogram embroidered in shades of silvery gray on a lapel. Marian blurted the news and then, like a second more devasting accident, Iris screamed. The harmony of her face broke up, distorted into an ugly tragic mask of pain. And I had a vision of the delicate peach-colored dress spattered with blood like a butcher's apron. The well-known image fell apart. The garden reeled, and, as though through a rent in my retina, I saw it reduced to a dot in a vast, threatening, agitated universe.

"Where is he?" she shouted.

Then the car turned around, heading for the gate on its way to the hospital. Later, when they returned, the report was good: Manfred had just been stunned, his back was uninjured, and he would be home the following day.

That evening when Iris descended the stairs for dinner, perfumed, wearing a gray chiffon negligée, the picture was restored. But in a double image the languid serene beauty of her face was accompanied by the ugly mask of tragedy. Her soft voice was a cover-up for that terrifying shriek and even the floating chiffon gown might be susceptible to splattered blood. I sensed the fragility of Eden, as evanescent and subject to sudden disappearance as the wings of the butterfly poised for a beautiful palpitating instant — glimpsed that morning, now eons ago.

Recurrent visits to Burlingame through the years of my growing up caused the double image of Iris's face to fade into the unreality of a bad dream. Her poise and grace became the reassurance they always had been. And Eden was temporarily restored. As I look back I see a gradual expulsion that had to do with accretion of time and the loss of that special vision of childhood through which we see the world objectively, if more dramatically colored than reality. Adolescence stands in its own light, and later, wonder is often replaced by reason. Burlingame was, after all, just another country house, and when it was sold after the death of "grandmother" Juliet and "great-aunt" Portia, I was occupied elsewhere and its disappearance was a matter of indifference. If it still exists and if I should see it again, even unchanged, I am sure I would not recognize it.

Iris survived into my adult life, a goddess in exile, as I never saw her again in her home setting. She enjoyed autumn in New York, and I recall walking with her on a brisk day, she sniffing the cold reviving air through her pink-lined nostrils like a thoroughbred released from its stall. "I do miss the seasons in San Francisco," she said, which made me realize that the East was Iris's home and the West only adopted through marriage.

Some summers we met in Paris, the city she loved above all others. She might have been a French *duchesse* strolling under the arcades, in the Tuileries Gardens, in the Bois, yet she remained an appreciative outlander, on home territory only at her dressmaker's, where she spent long hours in front of multiple mirrors being draped, pinned, and molded while the *vendeuse* fluttered obsequiously and the fitter kneeled at her feet. Once, as in a puberty rite, accompanied by Iris, I was permitted to buy a costume for myself. As far as I knew my mother had never entered one of these establishments and she was happy to turn me over to such expert guidance. I felt important but intimidated by the gilded white salon, like a novice page being introduced to the artificial intricacies of Versailles court life. I remember that I hastily selected a peacock-blue and black tweed suit and a hat with a shiny patent leather brim. Iris did not restrain me—perhaps it is impossible for a goddess to know what becomes a mortal. At any rate, when I tried on my French costume back home I was horrified by my reflection in bulky tweed, topped by a jutting black visor, a robot-like apparition. I never wore the ensemble, nor did I again visit a Parisian couturière with Iris. Her chic was inimitable, but I understood from the performance of that rite that if I were to discover my own, I would do it alone, without help.

After my mother's untimely death I saw Iris less frequently and our relationship was subtly altered. Her perfect exterior, alone, no longer interested me, and like a prospector I began to probe for the qualities that had meant so much to my mother. They were all there to be uncovered: her intelligence, sensitivity, even a quivering nervousness so like my mother's — but, in Iris, effectively masked by the elegant worldly image she projected. And sometimes, fleetingly, I felt that she was seeking my mother in me. But the timing was wrong, opportunities had been missed, the past was too strong and it overpowered the present. I was most at ease, after all, while admiring the perfect beauty of Iris without going deeper. At last, even she had to age. I noted that instinctively she sat with her back to the light in order to hide the lines and sagging of her face. Her hair untouched by silver now resembled brass rather than gold.

After her husband's death she often visited New York hoping to revive girlhood friendships. I knew that she deeply missed my mother and I felt my inadequacy as a substitute. Now that she was cut off from that special intimacy that extended back to her birth, I sensed her loneliness. Nevertheless a belated friendship burgeoned between us in spite of the difference in our ages. It was like an autumn rose, abnormal in its late blooming and destined to be short lived.

I recall one winter afternoon in my living room when Iris and I sat before a fire, she in a chair opposite me, her back still straight, barely grazing the cushion, her shapely legs crossed gracefully at the ankles — a characteristic pose — her face resolutely placed with the light behind her. She talked to me of her widowhood. "It is difficult to learn to walk all over again — alone — at sixty," she said. How little one understands others; it had never occurred to me that Iris was dependent on her husband, always a background figure for me. I had not yet arrived at the stage of comprehension of a long marriage: the slow growing together of two unlike human beings by a kind of natural erosion, until they come to form a single organism and the death of one is like an amputation. In spite of tinted hair, facial lines, and her sixty years, Iris seemed young, lost, broken — but not altogether hopeless. I sensed the possibility in her of new cycles of growth, discoveries, even surprises. But I could not guess what they would be.

I soon learned. In her sixties Iris found religion, the religion of her forebears deliberately forgotten by her generation and mine. Oh, I am certain that in the past she had dutifully attended the Reform Synagogue in San Francisco with old Juliet and Portia. But now Orthodox Judaism drew her. I pictured her inside a temple that preserved antiquity in archaic ritual, a place where the prophets hovered, not figures out of improbable myth, but real people out of history, distant kin ready to welcome home this prodigal, while her living relatives and her own children remained outside.

One morning Iris called me from San Francisco to tell me that she would be passing through New York the next day on her way to Israel. It seemed to me a pilgrimage to a far-off alien land, forbidding in its bare outlines of the Biblical past. The mistress of that paradisiacal garden in Burlingame, the sophisticated habituée of Parisian boulevards, was undertaking this long trip alone, despite her amputation. As she related her plans I detected a note of youthful hesitancy fortified by a new strong determination. One remark puzzled me; she said it was abnormally hot in San Francisco, rare for October. But the day happened to be in March.

Twenty-four hours later Marian telephoned to tell me that her mother had suffered a stroke. A few hours after Iris and I had spoken she had gone to the hairdresser in preparation for her departure. A cerebral accident had occurred while she was sitting under the dryer. The event came through to me in unbearable clarity: Iris's golden head trapped beneath the metal hood — it seemed to me that a beauty implement had turned into a lethal weapon. The goddess image, that she with the help of the rest of us had created, had proven fatal in the end. The bare bones of the land of Israel remained unknown to Iris. And for me, she was returned to that original Eden, the enclosed lush garden with the parched brown California hills outside the gate.

Iris died without regaining consciousness.

CHAPTER XIII

A Variety of
Religious Experience

A SENSE OF AWE is inborn in the human animal, as basic as the physical senses, as imperative as hunger or sex. The savage and the child accept this, but at various stages in history man has attempted to dominate it or obliterate it altogether by means of reason or scientific findings. Yet like a sleeping giant that sense of awe reasserts itself. In differing garb, using various vocabularies, the question posed through the ages is one, and the answer calls itself religion.

My father, the most reassuring and best-loved person in my childhood, was a militant atheist. He was neither a scientist nor a rationalist thinker; rather, he was like a comfortable Victorian family man with the latter's stuffy piety deleted. His father before him and his father before that, prosperous German and German-American brewers, were both disbelievers, a negative position they carried on blindly with the conviction of bigots. "Religion is a crutch for weaklings," I often heard my father remark. And he stepped out smartly with his polished cane always prepared to savor the quotidian. He was an urban type, and man-made wonders pleased him more than nature's. He gave his best attention to the aesthetics of grand boulevards and palaces. So it was by strange coincidence — or perhaps one of those prankish plans conceived by the unknown designer of our lives — that it was from the raised perch atop my father's shoulders that I became aware for the first time of the night sky.

One of my earliest memories, it happened in the summer, when we were staying, I believe, in the Austrian Tyrol. What my father and I were doing alone on that country lane at night, the occasion for my staying up so late, the reason for the disappearance of the rest of our traveling company — mother, brother, nurse, maid — I can no longer recall. Perhaps memory has chosen to edit them out of the text for reasons unknown to me. I am able to bring back the crunching sound of my father's feet on the stony path, unnaturally loud in the silence. I see the ghostly cones of haystacks, the commonplace product of Austrian industriousness by daylight. I smell the hay more delicate than the hearty odor baked by the sun. Most exactly, I feel again the roughness of my father's tweed jacket where my arms encircled his neck as we jogged along the country road. Was there a moon that night? If so, we would have cast an odd lumpy shadow: my father's short stature augmented by my slight shape growing from his shoulders like wings, one pair of legs transporting this double-headed apparition. The Tyrolean hills are gentle, but in the dark they crouched sphinxlike, while above them extended the immense sky perforated by the stars. As I stared up at them they lowered themselves toward me and began to grow, each into an infinite dazzling universe, while below everything receded and became uncertain. My father's footfalls and the German nursery rhyme he was humming tunelessly as we marched along sounded silly, helpless, tiny in the silence under the enormous nearness of the stars. Sky and earth revolved alarmingly. The position on my father's shoulders, so secure and triumphant a moment before, grew precarious. "I'm dizzy!" I cried, and was restored to the ground, reality regained as hand in hand my father and I retraced the way back to our hotel. It was past my time for bed.

I was unable to give a name to this experience and it was relegated to the back of my consciousness like a large useless piece of furniture in the attic.

During our European travels, chiefly organized by my father, we visited many churches. I am certain that he considered them only in the light of art objects or historical relics. High Gothic spires scraping the sky seemed to be made of lace imitating stone, and my father, an engineer, viewed their slender disproportion as achievements in construction. He appreciated the spans and buttresses that had allowed them to endure through centuries, but he ignored the faith that had created them and the hope still dwelling within. The interiors of churches were welcome to me because they were always dark, damp as wine cellars, and a relief after our hot strenuous sightseeing tours. I also felt at home because, after a welter of new impressions, they were all substantially the same. Filtered through stained-glass windows the light fell in prisms on old acquaintances that never lost their interest: the perpetually flickering candles on the altar, the crucifix, the statue of the Virgin — only an occasional offering of drooping flowers at her feet looked pathetic — and over all, the smell of accumulated incense. When we paid our visits to the churches they were empty, the pews deserted, and I could only imagine the pomp of a procession down the long aisles to the altar. Sometimes I spotted a solitary somber figure kneeling, head in hands, in all the vastness, every line of immobile body expressing submission and something else — a mystery. I would pause to look before my father ushered us outside into the glare of the sun. In time I associated those prostrated forms with something banished, vaguely embarrassing. But as with other mysteries, such as sex and death, I asked no questions and no explanations were offered.

In my childhood I viewed the Christian churches of Europe, Gothic, Roman, Baroque, Byzantine, but I never, even as a tourist, saw a synagogue. I was unaware of their existence. In Karlsbad, where my father took the cure, I would encounter on the streets a breed of men in dusty black robes, black pork-pie hats, and long curly side locks. They were pale, as though fresh air were a foreign element. I did ask about them and was told they were Polish Orthodox rabbis. Did I only imagine disgust in my father's voice? These men spoke an unintelligible language and they had the remoteness of unsightly foreigners, a flock of dingy birds from another planet.

As I grew up, my mother, a mild uncertain agnostic, proposed some kind of Bible instruction to temper the imperative of my father's atheism. But flanked by parents without faith I would have required an inspired leader to strike a spark in me. Instead, I was presented first with Miss Schwartz, a spinster of genteel aspect, and my lessons consisted of pasting colored pictures from the Old Testament into a scrapbook: Absalom hanging by his hair or Ruth among the "alien corn." Nothing remained from these lessons but the faint smell of glue. Miss Schwartz faded away and was replaced by James Wise. Although the son of a renowned Reform rabbi, Steven Wise, he preferred to think of himself as "free-thinking" and he had some connection with the Ethical Culture Society. He was a bull-necked young man with the broad shoulders of a football player, but my eyes were irresistibly attracted by the red socks he always wore, which drew my attention downward to his very large feet. And perhaps for this reason his face is lost to memory. We were a co-educational group of adolescents and met once a week in an apartment high up with a view of Central Park and the battlements of Fifth Avenue. Mr. Wise was "leftist," although our parents were unaware of this, and our sessions consisted of his heated monologues on the inequalities of capitalism, the problem of unemployment, and the promise of a socialist society. In all this, the Old Testament was lost. I see us, a disorganized, undisciplined, indolent crew with our thick-necked captain at the helm, invariably red-socked, steering us away from the dim receding shore line of our ancestors toward a new, classless, free-thinking world. In time, Mr. Wise disappeared also and here my formal religious education ended.

To a child reared without religion death is a taboo subject; robbed of dignity, it becomes an abnormality. Although in theory and in fact I was spared for many years, I was morbidly aware of death. But with the wiliness of the very young, I was adept at hiding this from my parents, who naively believed me to be protected. The only death in our family had been my grandfather's at ninety-one. It occurred during the summer when we were abroad, and although I had been fond of him, it barely touched me. His antiquity and our remoteness at the time caused the news to be as weightless as a dark cloud passing for a moment over the French beach where I had been playing.

But the sudden death of a mother of a Central Park acquaintance (a homely girl with thick lips and goggles, no intimate of mine) came as a shock. The information was inadvertently imparted in overheard whispered snatches from the governesses' bench and confirmed later by my mother, who did not believe it would be upsetting. Little did she realize that for me at that period death was not connected with personal loss, but existed, formidably, as a metaphysical nightmare. The fact that I scarcely knew the victim, a florid woman who presided over birthday parties, her hair worn in a high old-fashioned pompadour, did nothing to mitigate the horror. She had been here one day, living in a Park Avenue apartment like our own, the next day she had disappeared forever. Her daughter Mildred, though outwardly unchanged, became sinister, ill-omened, and I superstitiously averted my eyes from her. Many years later, long after she had been forgotten, I heard that she too had succumbed young to cancer. I experienced a pang of guilt as though my fear and avoidance of her, by some reverse process, had been an evil eye and was in some way responsible for her early death. She was brought up by a timid rabbity father, and though our mesdemoiselles remained close on their bench in the park, I refused to attend any more of her birthday parties. Her home was damned — I even turned away from its exterior and walked on the opposite side of the street. To this day the numbers on the apartment canopy spell an indelible message: death — sudden — overmastering — meaningless.

My parents persisted in the belief that their children were shielded. It was our duty to be happy and unworried. During the day I cooperated with them, but at night in bed, when my many small preoccupations had been set aside, I was often assailed by a wave of fear and impotence. Like genies, forbidden questions would arise: Why am I myself? What will I be when I'm dead? What was I before I was born? How did the world exist without me? (Very well.) Will it go on after me? (Without a doubt.) The utter insignificance of my life so camouflaged by daylight tricks would grow clear in the dark. Then a familiar chant, memorized in some other incarnation, sounded loudly in my ears: *I am nothing — come from nothing — going to nothing — I might have been a rock, a toad, a blade of grass . . .* In the blackness my bedroom grew strange and hostile, but I would not call for help because I knew that my mother's pale, sympathetic, frightened face would confirm my fears. And my father, totally uncomprehending, would merely say, "Don't be a little idiot!" But the idea of his stout words and the recall of his round bald head and swarthy familiar face with the small, wise, greenish eyes were comforting in themselves. And I would fall asleep at last, the incantation growing faint, routed by the thought of my father's presence.

When I was older my concern with the so-called ineffable diminished in proportion to my increased involvement with the so-called real. My father became less a comfort, an antidote, than an ally, until in his extreme old age, our roles reversing themselves, he became a charge. But his former self fought for survival, reappearing now and then like a nostalgic lovable ghost. As for the child in me, rarely brought out in the open, it persisted also: submerged in some dark recess of my being it would, in all likelihood, be preserved as long as my body endured. When the end came at last for my father, I was privileged to witness his dealings with the enemy. In spite of age and illness he was able to savor what remained of each sadly reduced day. He faced extinction squarely, with utmost regret but without a trace of visible fear. And as in my youth, the unshakable atheist, the hedonistic wise man made his appearance once again.

It often happens that adults, confident that they are emancipated and are overthrowing the thralldom of the past by not repeating the errors of their parents, unwittingly imitate the very situations they believe they are avoiding. And history repeats itself inexorably. I was determined that my son's religious education should be different from my own; he should be acquainted with his roots and take pride in them. With this in mind we consulted Dr. Abraham Joshua Heschel, whose books my husband published. He was a Conservative rabbi, head of the Department of Mysticism at the Jewish Theological Seminary in New York City. He was a short, stocky man who spoke with a guttural Polish accent, and I found him slightly obsequious. I was aware that, although he dressed in an ordinary suit, he was kin to those black-frocked Middle Eastern rabbis I had passed on the streets of Karlsbad. Priding myself on the overcoming of my father's prejudices, I took pains in the planning of kosher meals for Dr. Heschel's occasional visits, while remaining inattentive to his words and unimpressed by the serenity in his dark eyes.

Dr. Heschel selected Everett Gendler, his most promising pupil, for my son's instruction, and Everett proved to be all that one could wish. He had the surprising rosy beauty of an angel in a painting by Fra Angelico, and a nimbus of fair hair. Even my father would have been impressed by his appearance. And his irradiant dedication was quite contagious. I almost envied my son's privilege, taking no notice of the fact that he was, as I had once been, flanked by unbelieving parents, and that it is difficult for faith to take root in barren soil. Sometimes I would eavesdrop on the lesson, always I was moved and interested, yet nothing changed in my life pattern: I sought no further religious education for myself and the synagogue remained uncharted territory. In retrospect my listening in on those sessions appears like an adult assisting at a nursery supper, who, sampling it, finds it quite delicious but, after all, child's fare. After confirmation we lost track of Everett Gendler. Our son went on to an Episcopalian boarding school and religion played no more part in his life than in his parents'. Yet I persisted in thinking complacently that I had performed my duty, and above all I felt that I had purged myself of my father's didactic atheism.

I rarely saw Dr. Heschel, although later he did introduce us to a young Irish Jesuit in revolt against the Church. They had met at Pope John's Ecumenical Congress and my husband's firm published Father Gerard's heretical pseudonymous book alongside the pious Jewish philosophical writings of Dr. Heschel. My first meeting with Father Gerard took place in Paris on a bleak, damp winter's day. He came into the lobby of our hotel, a slender sparrow of a man, still wearing the priestly collar and a thin black suit. A narrow white scarf flung around his neck and short leather gloves were his only protection against the cold. In the cordon bleu restaurant, surrounded by succulent joints, hors d'oeuvres displayed as jewels, a dessert wagon laden with creamy sweets, billowy and overflowing as a cornucopia, Father Gerard appeared a true ascetic, contenting himself with a sliver of boiled white fish and an apple. But his endless monologue spilling out in a faintly Irish brogue was another overflowing cornucopia. He had lived in the Middle East, was learned in Semitic history, and spoke seven languages fluently. His culture was remote from mine but I was nevertheless impressed, as once I had been among the symbolic ornaments inside the dusky Catholic cathedrals visited in my youth.

Father Gerard arrived in the United States. He continued to write audacious books on religious subjects, now under his true name as his connection with the Order had been severed. He formed an attachment to a wealthy Egyptian divorcée, a friend of ours, presiding over her table, becoming intimately involved with all her family, a little above mundane matters but fully equipped to deal with them as though to the manner born. I marveled at the physical metamorphosis that gradually took place in him. I would observe him pouring the wine, the slender sparrow superseded by this substantial man in well-tailored evening attire. The hand, thick as a ham, pouring the golden or ruby liquid, seemed as large as the entire person I remembered sitting before his meager fish in the Parisian restaurant. He was host at Elena's banquets, consort in her worldly schemes, a connoisseur of her dusky beauty and her jewels. He still held forth on philosophical subjects, his garrulousness unchecked by his new exterior. But now megalomania was apparent in his words and in his massive classical head like a Roman emperor's touched by madness. He talked on and on, predicting the death of Jesus in the contemporary Christian world and the end of all formal religions, hinting at the formation of a new merged faith for which he, Gerard, would be the catalyst.

He and Dr. Heschel had long since parted company. I no longer remember the direct cause for their quarrel. The rabbi and the lapsed priest were like a divorced couple and, accordingly, though convinced of Gerard's unsoundness, we continued to see him and Elena rather than Dr. Heschel. From time to time I would read in the newspaper about Dr. Heschel's opposition to the Vietnam war or see a photograph of him marching with civil rights protestors. He had grown long white hair and a flowing beard, which caused a participant at Selma to exclaim, "Dere is de Lawd!" Occasionally I had news of him through my husband: another book was to be published, he was going to Rome for a conference with Pope Paul, he had had a severe heart attack and had recovered, resuming his studies, his writing, his meditations and, in spite of his damaged heart, his unstinting battle against the world's wrongdoings.

Not long ago, we were invited to attend a ceremonial luncheon in his honor at the Waldorf Astoria. The converted ballroom was packed. My father's daughter, I viewed the crowd with suspicion, denying my identification with it. Our table was composed of corpulent businessmen, their bellies bulging out of loud sport shirts, accompanied by their overdressed wives. The perimeter of the white cloth might have been the shore line of Miami Beach. Interspersed among these oily benefactors were the rabbis, pale and learned, wearing skull caps and side locks. I could not understand their Talmudic abstractions and did not wish to join the others in their large monetary boasts. I looked around and saw our table multiplied by the hundreds all around the huge room.

On the dais the distinguished Hebrew scholars and religionists were more impressive. In their center I located Dr. Heschel and his wife. But he was almost unrecognizable! While Gerard had inflated, Dr. Heschel had dwindled. His white head with flowing hair and beard seemed too large to be supported by his frail body. He did not seem to be his sixty-odd years but nearer eighty. The worshipful testimonial speeches were over, and at last Dr. Heschel rose, accepting the medal with humility. He began to speak in a weak, reedy voice. His words are lost; perhaps I never heard them, because a phenomenon was taking place. The small figure of Dr. Heschel (one more link in an endless chain stretching backward in time to Abraham) slowly levitated before my eyes. It dangled like a puppet from invisible strings, lifted off the floor above the crowd and the long speaker's table on the dais. His body, held up by a hidden power, was suspended for I don't know how long before my vision (if it was that) broke. Dr. Heschel was seated again and we filed out of the room, down in the elevator to the street outside the Waldorf Astoria. But that sight was still with me and it returned many times during the following months. With neither emotion nor comprehension I saw again the dangling prophet-puppet. A real event, it gave me no rest. Like a scientist, I must discover its cause. Was it possible that it had been a mere hallucination engendered by regret at having wasted so many opportunities to know a great man, remorse for my Jewish anti-Semitism, a late rebellion again submission to my father's dictums, an unsatisfied yearning for religion? Whatever it was, it must be verified, and I realized that Dr. Heschel would be the means.

One Sunday morning I called to invite him and his wife for dinner. He answered the telephone himself, sounding gay, almost bantering, delighted to see us again after so long. His tone was a satisfaction. Had he been solemn and rabbinical the indelible memory of that scene at the Waldorf might have been reduced to some pious trickery. But his unpretentious, buoyant words reinforced the reality of what I had seen. Levitation is an act of lightness, Dr. Heschel had been liberated from terrestrial weightiness, despite his deep involvement in the world's ills. The selection of him as worthy of this supernatural support was a component in my secret experiment.

The night before our meeting was to take place I was roused from deep sleep by the ringing of the telephone. An unfamiliar girlish voice said, "I am Suzannah Heschel." I was about to hang up, thinking it was a wrong number, when she continued, "I am Dr. Heschel's daughter. My father died this afternoon." She went on with information concerning funeral arrangements. I pitied the young stricken voice but frustration and rage prevented me from heeding the details. The vial that had contained the precious ingredients had been shattered! Now no conclusion would ever be reached. I lay wakeful in the dark and, as in my childhood, it was growing hostile. But the comforting thought of my father was gone. At that moment I remembered him with resentment, as though all along we had been locked in combat and now, many years dead, he was the victor. The silence pulsed with messages: one of them promised, "tomorrow . . . there are more mysteries, unsuspected discoveries, and much unfinished business . . ."

CHAPTER XIV

Götterdämmerung

ALTHOUGH I LEARNED to diagnose the symptoms of hero-worship in myself, it was new — one more jolt out of child-hood — to recognize, objectively, the process in others. One night at a party at Rhinebeck I became an observer, and this episode and, later, the ordeal of my brother's terminal illness are associated in memory like theater masks: comic and tragic, which together express for me a common meaning.

The house of Frederick Dupee, Columbia professor and writer, and his wife, Andy, looked out from a pleasant valley onto a broad passage of the Hudson River. It was romantic, evocative of the past, but unlike the home of Stanley and Nancy Young, an Eastern temple, or Finistère, a French import, this place was indigenously American. Over the sweep of uncultivated land stretching to the river I could picture a band of Indians running toward the horizon. The Hudson was revealed in a large triangle between the cleavage of the shore. It had grown from the ribbon that bordered Manhattan Island to a body of water as wide as a lake. For some reason, in the fading light of dusk it reminded me of Mark Twain's Mississippi, and I expected a paddle-wheel boat to appear within the triangular vista.

The house itself was peculiarly American also, high-gabled, shabby but splendid, as haunting as the setting for a tale by Hawthorne. Fred Dupee, out of Wisconsin, for years a member of a group of New York City intellectuals, fully appreciated the romance of his home. The Hudson Valley still echoed with its history, fast fading, but audible to him who knew how to listen and see with his imagination. When he first became owner of the Rhinebeck house he had talked enthusiastically about his neighbors, descended from the original settlers, calling them the "river people." They sounded like water sprites, but when I met one of the species she turned out to be an octogenarian, wispy as a cobweb. He introduced her to my husband as though presenting a young beauty and escorted her ceremoniously on his arm into dinner as if she were the duchesse de Guermantes and he the Marcel Proust of the early Combray years.

This night, however, the leading player was to be of a different sort. Our host met us at the door and told us about a Mr. Tailor, whom we had not met before. "He is fabulous — you'll see. He has just moved into the area — a millionaire many times over, self-made, now a top executive in utilities. He was born in Hungary and has Americanized his name. His parties are right out of the *Arabian Nights*, under a pink marquee, with enough champagne to fill an ocean . . ."

I had a vision this time of the Great Gatsby, updated and transplanted from the manicured Long Island shore to the Gothic wildness of the Hudson Valley.

The rest of the guests were known and part of the Dupees' customary entourage. There was Philip Rahv, editor and critic. His presence was always pleasing to me. Although he was as swarthy and bulky as a Russian peasant, he never ceased to seem inappropriate to the rural settings he loved. His soft, kind, ruminating brown eyes gave the lie to the corrosive brilliance of his mind, and he had an insatiable avidity for gossip. "Tell me what's new," he would demand, every large feature in his heavy face alert to receive the tidbit I would throw him like a piece of raw meat. He would receive it with appetite, exclaiming, *"Please!"* at some disclosure, while he ran his paw through his black hair in consternation, "it's too much!"

That night the critic Dwight Macdonald and his wife Gloria were also included. Dwight, an enthusiastic talker, was a major key accompaniment to the gloomy minor of Philip Rahv. While Philip muttered and groaned, Dwight insisted loudly and guffawed. He had a pointed grisly beard and animated eyes behind spectacles. His conversation cavorted and stamped; at times he reminded me of a clever jester imitating the capers of a billy goat.

Gore Vidal was there, looking aristocratic and disdainful, and Chanler Chapman, son of the renowned writer John J. Chapman. He carried his family tradition like an overpowering load, too heavy even for his strong shoulders. He might have been classified as a "river person," having been reared beside the Hudson he had never deserted, but he was taken by the Dupees as part of the usual blend. Dressed in blue jeans, he certainly did not resemble the now departed octogenarian "river lady" I recalled in her refined chiffon ruffles and heirloom jewelry.

There were others besides, unremarkable for a party at the Dupees', and I no longer remember which of the regular band they were. Fred led me up to Mr. Tailor, murmuring, "You're going to adore him. I have seated you next to him." Mr. Tailor was tall and handsome in a Slavic way. Only his neat navy-blue business suit and starched white shirt resembled an American banker's and made the plaids, reds, purples, madras, and corduroy jackets of the other guests look as disorderly and colorful as a neglected garden of common zinnias. Our conversation began inauspiciously with his proclaiming himself a "hawk." The Vietnam war was as necessary in his view as World War II, and the Communist threat as dire as Hitler. I attempted to divert him into other channels, searching for the qualities heralded by Fred, but Mr. Tailor would have none of it. Surrounded by the retired army of the anti-McCarthyites, he was anachronistically still fighting the Cold War. I seemed to see him limned against the red, white, and blue of the American flag. He was shouting now, "So you are one of those pro-Hitler types — an isolationist! — unappreciative of the privileges of your marvelous country! I tell you it's worth fighting for. I will never stop being grateful for the opportunities it has given me . . ." I could only long for dinner to be over so that I could escape. Suddenly, in the middle of his tirade, Mr. Tailor paused and without preamble asked, "Which one is Dwight Macdonald? Point him out to me."

I searched the islands of tables scattered around the high-ceilinged drawing room, dining room, and entrance hall. Shadows lurked in dark corners filled with the dreams and the hush of the past, not to be routed by the noisy garrulousness of the present company. I located Dwight shouting at his dinner partner. He was sweating and mopping his bearded face with a napkin, but he appeared to be enjoying himself immensely as he countered all opposition with the fly swatter of his shrill words accompanied by his high-pitched laughter. After the ominous proximity of Mr. Tailor, Dwight looked as endearing as a boisterous child at a birthday party, and in my mind's eye I supplied him with a cocked paper hat and a cardboard whistle.

I indicated him to Mr. Tailor, who studied him in silence, drawing his heavy dark brows together until they met across his nose, and dinner being over I fled from his side. But I continued to observe him throughout the evening. He was growing drunk and more menacing, his dark suit a lone storm cloud. Later, as I was sitting with Dwight Macdonald, he approached. His step tipsy but determined, he stopped, towering before the unsuspecting Dwight. Mr. Tailor's glowering expression cut off Dwight's copious flow of words and his loud laughter. "So you are Dwight Macdonald," he said with cold fury. "I am going to kill you." And seizing him by the lapels he started to shake him, as though Dwight's considerable size were no more than a small rabbit's.

A crowd had gathered around. Dwight was pale between his whiskers and Mr. Tailor seemed to be rapidly growing larger. "I am going to kill you," he repeated. And in the moment before the two men, locked together as one, were separated, I believed him.

I watched as Fred Dupee, aided by some others, detached Mr. Tailor from the shocked Dwight and escorted him, fighting all the way, across the room, to the door through which he was ejected from the house. Dwight tucked his crumpled plaid shirt back into his trousers and reknotted his tie. Fred returned with profuse apologies. He had a look of bewilderment and hurt in his electric blue eyes, with which I could identify. I felt a new closeness to him and, strangely, some understanding also of the departed Mr. Tailor.

I sympathized with Fred's glorification of this man, so different from him and his friends. But the royal mantle he had bestowed upon Mr. Tailor did not belong to him; it was Fred's creation — in tatters now. As he continued to apologize to Dwight and me I was saddened by the thought that Fred would no longer be privileged to attend those parties beneath the pink marquee where the champagne flowed like the sea — and if he should, I knew that the tent would be merely the equipment of a parvenu and the champagne would have a bitter taste.

And what about Mr. Tailor? No less than Fred, no less than I, he too in his own way was a romantic. An outsider, he felt that his pile of gold was being tarnished by the hot breath of the intellectuals. Mr. Tailor had selected Dwight Macdonald as their king. And pricked by his ego, goaded by his own imagination, he was out to kill, like a bull at the sight of the red cape.

The party was over. I realized that the Dupees considered it a failure and I didn't know how to tell them what it meant to me. Outside the cool air was a relief. The dew-drenched grass extended darkly, immaterial as a shadow. The Hudson illuminated by a full moon was paler and looked more solid than the land. It was late August, and with the new season we would soon all meet again in the city. I looked back at the high-gabled silhouette of the house, trying to memorize its outline. It rose peacefully against the night sky. But the windows blazed and I was certain that were I to return within I would find a scene of destruction smelling sharply of fire and brimstone.

The Brother

"IT REMINDS ME of the Beverly Hills Hotel," my brother had said upon his arrival at the nursing home in lower Connecticut. He knew better later, as did I, but though he was damaged and paralyzed, the will to impose his desires on reality still flourished in him. The route I took to visit him at the nursing home soon assumed the hideousness of a passage to hell.

But months before that there had been the hospital way, the third circle. I turned sharply at a shopping center: parking area, supermarket, ten-cent store, and movie theater met me like fire-breathing monsters guarding the gate. A steep decline came out on the throughway, with its perpetual roar, and the hospital loomed on a hill above the noise.

My brother was in the intensive care ward. He had been found the night before unconscious in his car. He now lay, putty-colored, his eyes sealed, his elongated body utterly still. Only his lips moved rhythmically in a tiny sucking motion that reminded me of an infant dreaming of the nipple. A network of wires and tubes attached to a battery of bottles was pumping false life into him: the victim was to be aroused to purgatory. Although he appeared to be deep under layers of oblivion, he feebly returned the pressure of my hand and his peaceful eyelids fluttered like trapped moths as, thickly, he uttered my name.

Removed from the ward to a private room, my brother fought his way back to awareness. The doctors held out little hope of his walking again, and he would never regain the use of his left arm. Still in his fifties, he would be a complete cripple if he survived. I sat beside the high bed with iron sides like a crib and he tried to talk in that new thick voice of his. We had never had anything to say to one another but now I longed for his voluble monologues, invariably on topics distasteful to me: the world of advertising, big business, his shaky money transactions, sprinkled over with the sugar of sentimental recollections from our shared childhood which always made me wince. Now I missed my brother and wished he would return to replace this mumbling stranger. His inert body was covered by the hospital sheet, only his emaciated head emerged with his jutting nose and twisted mouth that looked as though it had been in the path of a tornado. In the reversal of our roles I now did most of the talking while he responded with difficulty, his eyes closed as though it were necessary to concentrate all his senses into the enormous effort of forming words — when before his illness he had used them as a tidal wave to break down all resistance to his will. At intervals I glanced at my watch counting the slow minutes to release.

The doctors came and went, their essential powerlessness

imperfectly concealed by their masks of wisdom. After weeks it was decided to move the inert mass from the hospital bed to the rigors of a rehabilitation center. Now I moved in another orbit: the second circle. On the way a country cemetery clamored for one more tenant. A broad road was interspersed with stop lights, winking red and green, sparks from a greater hidden fire. The Center, a gray stone mansion, was set in a spacious park. Over the grass, still in summer green, beneath the shade trees aflame with autumn, no soul wandered. Within, the ghastly army of the crippled were kept busy with the routine of their barracks existence, in ignorance of the outdoors as it beckoned, lovely but forbidden — part of the upper world from which they had been banished. There was a stately staircase leading to the main entrance as though it belonged to a campus building: a senior class should have been posed there for a graduation photograph. Instead it was deserted, except for a few visitors like me. In the echoing front hall there was a cluster of wheelchairs containing grandmothers surrounded by generations of their families; children were not permitted further as they might disrupt the rigid military discipline. In front of an arched window as high as a church's, banks of flowers were displayed, changing with the seasons: chrysanthemums in the fall, poinsettias at Christmas, and lilies for Easter.

Upstairs, by contrast, everything was scrupulously plain, stripped of color and any attempt at decoration. On my first visit after emerging from the elevator I was confronted by a line-up of wheelchairs. Strapped to them were the soldiers of this institution, a bedraggled lot, listing this way and that despite their supports. I scanned the faces and the contorted bodies for the familiar one. They were of various ages. A young girl barely out of her teens had the long fall of hair worn by the current "hippies"; under an army blanket her legs were useless. A man with bulging ebony cheek revealed a robust torso ending in two stumps. A middle-aged housewife, a coquettish dyed blonde with a withered face over which her features wandered awry, twitched regularly beneath her cover. There were many others, ranged for the next command. "They're just down from the gymnasium," an attendant informed me. In the front rank, a gaunt figure slipped sideways in his chair. He had a scrawny wrinkled neck, gray stubble on his narrow cheeks and chin, and one arm in a sling; he raised the other long-fingered El Greco hand in salutation. It was my brother.

In the beginning he complained without cease in his blurred voice. The exertions in the gymnasium would kill him, he was too long for the institution bed, there were not enough nurses to go round. He was using pull to return to the comforts of the hospital which had now assumed for him the coziness of the womb. But as the weeks passed he began, like a patriotic recruit, to be proud of his activities. He urged me over and over to visit the sessions in the gymnasium. "You have never seen anything like it," he insisted. "We all help each other and we are as delighted with each other's progress as with our own. When someone goes down the ramp without assistance everyone claps."

He had been fitted with a ponderous brace: foot to thigh, leather and iron, buckled and screwed, it cut viciously into his leg. He was always eager to demonstrate his improvement, but when he wavered, shuffled, and clanked down the hall, his six-and-a-half-foot bent frame supported by two attendants, he resembled a skeleton called up again for active duty in the army of the dead.

The day arrived when I was summoned to an interview with the director. I had never met him but my brother had told me that he had the bearing of a Prussian officer. When Dr. Schmitt visited the gymnasium my brother would attempt to stand up straight and with his good arm he would salute in military fashion. *"Guten Tag, Herr General,"* he would say. This seemed to afford him satisfaction because he often repeated it with undiminished relish. On the descending graph of a dying patient the insignificant up-swings are as outstanding as the heights achieved in normal living.

Dr. Paul Schmitt's office was small but trim. Everywhere there was evidence of his holiday hobby: sailing. There were pictures of sloops and yawls, an inkstand in the shape of a steering wheel, a paperweight adorned with knots of rope — altogether the taste of a healthy outdoors man and an insult to the maimed bodies in his charge. His person, too, appeared to have resisted pity with the adroitness of an athlete. His step was staccato, his back perfectly erect, his shoulders smartly held, his complexion ruddy-tan, weathered by salt spray. His voice was firm and expressionless as, looking at me directly with his sea-blue eyes, he said, "We have done all we can for your brother. He will never get better. The next move — right now — is the nursing home." I was dismissed, and as Dr. Schmitt ushered me out I felt that he considered it a breach of army etiquette that, unlike my brother, I had failed to salute.

The nursing home was as synthetic as a motel: hollow Neoclassical columns on the exterior, and inside, artificial flowers, pseudo-antique pewter chandeliers, thick imitation

Persian carpets, and throughout, the chemical chill of air-conditioning. If the Rehabilitation Center had been a barracks, this was a camouflaged cemetery. Here the inhabitants were frozen into extreme old age, and well-fed inertness replaced the painful efforts at the Center. Hopelessness, the anesthetic of those interred while still alive, held sway. My brother was the lone comparatively young member of this society. Although convivial by nature, he refused to mingle with the other patients, preferring to remain inside his chintzy bedroom, like the moribund I glimpsed through their open doors. One old woman lay motionless on her back, open-mouthed; near her shriveled head a canary trilled in its cage. She seemed to be drinking up the tiny notes as though they were drops of life-prolonging medicine.

I would find my brother stretched on his bed, the heavy brace discarded in a corner of the room like a soldier's equipment dropped after the war is over. His bony legs were lost inside his old trousers, which had to be held up by suspenders. His paralyzed arm was now shrouded in a cast as though it had received a separate, premature burial. With his woolly, shaggy, graying hair, his narrow head, and stick-like limbs, he reminded me of an aging wolfhound. Now he implored me to help him to return to the Rehabilitation Center. When once he had longed for the comforts of the hospital, he was now nostalgic for the active life of the barracks and his colleagues there. Characteristically, he bombarded the Center with telephone calls and dictated daily letters to the director. But Dr. Schmitt remained firm; he ran a taut outfit and a permanently disabled soldier never returned. My brother remained in the luxury-motel-cemetery: the first circle of hell. But he did not give up easily.

He still strained for outside employment, even having himself hoisted by derrick on and off airplanes en route to Detroit, Cleveland, or Chicago. He made me spread out on the floor of the nursing home dining room long rolls of colored posters, advertisements for breweries. The ambulatory, senile ladies arriving for the big event of their day — lunch or supper — would step around the photographic display of castles on the Rhine like tottering tourists surveying mosaics with gummy, unappreciative eyes. The Brewers Association presented my brother with an inscribed brass plaque of commendation. I hoped that he saw the reflection of his twisted face in its polished surface, rather than in the mirror over the bureau. Now I encouraged him in his business endeavors. For the first time I listened with sympathy and patience to his grandiose schemes, while continuing to glance surreptitiously at my watch.

But his rapidly dwindling energies grew more and more directed toward the Rehabilitation Center. His desire for it was becoming a mania. "If only I could go back there, I know I would be able to walk again," he said, adding unexpectedly, "— because of Anna."

"Who is Anna?" I asked.

"Who is Anna — " he repeated. "An angel of mercy, a madonna, a beautiful young girl — she will come to me — she has done so much for me. I have written her a note of thanks. She used to stand next to the ramp in the gymnasium when I was waiting for my turn, and although she didn't even know my name, she would murmur words of encouragement to me. If I could just see her . . . She wasn't strictly speaking beautiful — short, stocky, strong, with curly black hair and black eyes. She looked like an Italian peasant girl, but to me . . ." He mumbled on and on. "I never really spoke to her," he continued. "I didn't even find out her last name, but I feel I've known her always . . ." My brother's three wives, divorced and forgotten, no longer existed inside his sick brain, filled to overflowing by this stranger.

He extracted a crumpled paper from a pocket of his shirt. "Find her and give her this from me," he said. "She will know how to take me back there."

All at once I found myself shouting, "You fool! Are you crazy? You don't know her and she's unaware of your existence. You can never go back — do you hear? *Never, never*, do you understand?"

He winced as though I had struck him and returned the paper to his pocket. But, knowing him, I was sure he had not given up.

Flushed and shaken, I rose to leave before the usual hour. As though pursued by the devil I fled along the thickly carpeted corridors, smelling of corrupting flesh and disinfectant, past the reception desk, the fake flowers, the heavy hanging pewter chandelier out into the sunny, steamy parking lot.

Safely inside my car, I took stock of my strange behavior. What had possessed me to be so cruel to that hopeless-hopeful wreck on his chintz-covered tomb? The faint smell of gasoline in the car seemed to be merging with the fumes from an ether cone and I was transported back to the nursery of my childhood, converted into a hospital for my brother's and my tonsillectomies. As a reward for the ordeal he was to receive an expensive toy hook-and-ladder car he coveted. When asked what I wanted, I had replied,

"Nothing." At six, it was already my ambition to resemble in no way my awkward, humorless, spoiled, hysterical, unhappy brother. And although I had looked with longing at a life-sized wax infant doll in a shop window, I gave my answer in opposition to him and against my desire. Before the thick, sweet, choking fumes and the colored kaleidoscopic visions of ether overwhelmed me, I had thought: I am not like him — I never will be — he is not my brother.

Now with the smell of gasoline-ether in my nostrils, I discovered the cause for my senseless fury. As in a distorting mirror I had glimpsed myself reflected in my brother. Anna, the stocky therapist at the Rehabilitation Center, a beautiful angel of mercy was related to my own personal creations, stretching back over so many years to the Lunts, early gods of my childhood.

Epilogue

When I left the museum, the period wax dummies, along with the drug exhibition, rapidly disappeared from the horizon of my mind. I strolled down Fifth Avenue on the Central Park side. Under an arcade of trees other pedestrians moved before me in a long file. Here and there above their heads, red balloons bobbed — in perspective, the size of cherries. Bemused, I was buoyed up by the crowd, as undifferentiated as the patterns of a thousand faces adorning my mother's Chinese porcelain tea set. I used to be hypnotized by the miniature, pointillist, multitudinous population swarming around the fragile contour of a cup.

As I passed Eighty-sixth Street I looked inside the park searching in vain for a particular young mother pushing her son in his pram. Dr. Buchanan's obstetrical magic still fresh in memory, she was lonely for her husband far off somewhere in the unknown Pacific. A battery of new mothers and prams had replaced her and there were no impressions of her feet or her baby's carriage wheels left behind on the hard asphalt paths.

At the Seventy-second Street entrance the garlanded horses and buggies still plodded their way westward. But the Casino-in-the-Park, that temple of love where Skinny reigned, a god, had been razed a generation ago. I was no longer certain of its precise location.

The transverse at Sixty-sixth Street, the route to Lincoln Center, crawled with busses. But Vincent Sheean, a portly, aging Odysseus returned from his voyages, was no longer going to and fro to hear the arias of the divas, as seductive and beckoning as the strains of the Sirens.

At the Zoo, the ghost of Father Teilhard de Chardin hovered palely, a transparency of itself. And as I glimpsed the Plaza down the avenue, I could no longer recall even the outline of that person who had sat on the rim of the fountain, in a holiday mood, with her sad-comic, Chaplinesque friend Charles Jackson by her side.

The showcases of memory are not immortal, although the hero-worshiper, a misguided mystic, is always searching for a fragment of the divine in the human scene. Like a pagan, he sets up idols — in this likeness or that. As I write these lines I am aware that this early religion exists in me still — but flickeringly, in twilight. What will the new day bring?